Management Extra

MANAGING FOR RESULTS

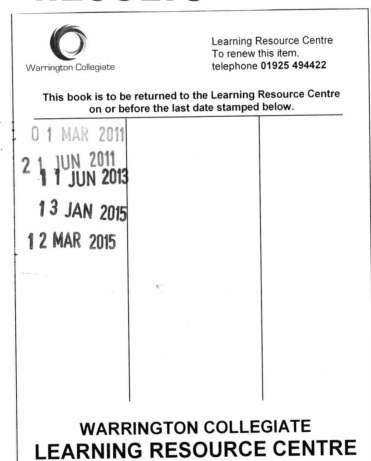

Management Extra

MANAGING FOR RESULTS

ELSEVIER

eLEARN

Pergamon
Flexible
Learning

AMSTERDAM • BOSTON • HEIDELBERG • LONDON • NEW YORK • OXFORD • PARIS •
SAN DIEGO • SAN FRANCISCO • SINGAPORE • SYDNEY • TOKYO

Pergamon Flexible Learning is an imprint of Elsevier
Linacre House, Jordan Hill, Oxford OX2 8DP, UK
30 Corporate Drive, Suite 400, Burlington, MA 01803, USA

First published 2005
Revised edition 2009

British Library Cataloguing in Publication Data
A catalogue record for this book is available from the British Library

Library of Congress Cataloging-in-Publication Data
A catalog record for this book is available from the Library of Congress

ISBN 978-0-08-055746-5

Printed and bound in Hungary

Contents

List of activities   vii

List of figures   viii

List of tables   ix

Series preface   xi

Introduction: motivation and improvement   xiii

1 Specify the results   1

The context for managing results   1

Clarifying the results that are required   8

Recap   13

More @   13

2 Motivation theory   15

The importance of motivation   15

Key motivation theories   19

Recap   30

More @   31

3 Motivation to achieve results   32

Motivation in practice   32

Creating the conditions for results management   47

Linking rewards and results   58

Recap   69

More @   70

4 Grievance and disciplinary procedures   72

The grievance process and links to results management   72

The disciplinary process and links to results management   86

Recap   99

More @   100

5 A balancing act   102

Balancing needs and achieving results   102

Recap   114

More @   114

References   115

Activities

Activity 1   Having an impact on results   6

Activity 2   Setting up and managing tasks   11

Activity 3   Maslow's hierarchy of needs   26

Activity 4   Herzberg's satisfiers and dissatisfiers   28

Activity 5   Motivation in the workplace   40

Activity 6   The meaning of motivation   41

Activity 7   Team motivational and performance survey   44

Activity 8   Working conditions   56

Activity 9   Rewards   66

Activity 10   Rewarding the team   68

Activity 11   Grievance handling   80

Activity 12   Dissatisfaction, complaint or grievance?   84

Activity 13   Discipline   96

Activity 14   Balancing needs and achieving results   111

Figures

1.1	The basic results management process	2
1.2	The context for results management	2
1.3	The uncertainty map	10
2.1	Basic motivational model	16
2.2	Maslow's hierarchy of needs	20
2.3	Basic model of expectancy theory	24
2.4	Locke's theory of goal setting	25
2.5	Maslow's hierarchy of needs	26
3.1	A model of job enrichment	35
3.2	Leadership in teams	37
3.3	Sales director's responsibilities	60
4.1	Outline disciplinary procedure	88
5.1	The range of needs managers must meet	102
5.2	The leadership continuum	104
5.3	Interaction to get results	105

Tables

2.1 The relationship between job satisfaction and employee turnover   16

2.2 Indicators of motivation at work   19

2.3 Determinants of satisfaction and dissatisfaction   22

4.1 Understanding grievance   73

5.1 Characteristics of a team briefing   109

Series preface

Whether you are a tutor/trainer or studying management development to further your career, Management Extra provides an exciting and flexible resource helping you to achieve your goals. The series is completely new and up-to-date, and has been written to harmonise with the 2004 national occupational standards in management and leadership. It has also been mapped to management qualifications, including the Institute of Leadership & Management's middle and senior management qualifications at Levels 5 and 7 respectively on the revised national framework.

For learners, coping with all the pressures of today's world, Management Extra offers you the flexibility to study at your own pace to fit around your professional and other commitments. Suddenly, you don't need a PC or to attend classes at a specific time – choose when and where to study to suit yourself! And, you will always have the complete workbook as a quick reference just when you need it.

For tutors/trainers, Management Extra provides an invaluable guide to what needs to be covered, and in what depth. It also allows learners who miss occasional sessions to 'catch up' by dipping into the series.

This series provides unrivalled support for all those involved in management development at middle and senior levels.

Reviews of Management Extra

I have utilised the Management Extra series for a number of Institute of Leadership and Management (ILM) Diploma in Management programmes. The series provides course tutors with the flexibility to run programmes in a variety of formats, from fully facilitated, using a choice of the titles as supporting information, to a tutorial based programme, where the complete series is provided for home study. These options also give course participants the flexibility to study in a manner which suits their personal circumstances. The content is interesting, thought provoking and up-to-date, and, as such, I would highly recommend the use of this series to suit a variety of individual and business needs.

Martin Davies BSc(Hons) MEd CEngMIMechE MCIPD FITOL FInstLM
Senior Lecturer, University of Wolverhampton Business School

At last, the complete set of books that make it all so clear and easy to follow for tutor and student. A must for all those taking middle/senior management training seriously.

Michael Crothers, ILM National Manager

Motivation and improvement

This book looks at how to get the best out of people and celebrate the diversity of perspectives and experience that people bring to your organisation. It covers these key questions:

◆ Can you deal with the conflicting demands that affect your productivity?

◆ How motivated are you and your team?

◆ Can you use incentives wisely and deal with poor performance?

Get results

To be able to deliver the results required of you and your team, you need to understand how to help people get the best out of themselves in work settings. Managing for results is an integral part of the manager's role. There are plenty of theories and war stories to guide us, but rarely are we given a clear route to achieving excellence in this role.

Our own experiences tell us that we work best when goals are clear, we are able to contribute in ways that boost our confidence, are happy and can see that our efforts contribute to both the results required and the well-being of colleagues. By developing your awareness and skills in these areas you will improve your ability to achieve results with your team.

Your objectives are to:

◆ Contribute more effectively to the overall goals and objectives of your unit and the organisation

◆ Develop an understanding of how individuals and teams harness motivation to achieve results

◆ Identify how individual expectations affect performance

◆ Explore the nature of the rewards that individuals expect and link them to the results that are expected of them

◆ Explore new ways of balancing the varying needs of individuals and the team when managing for results.

1   Specify the results

Many of us get the job done, but we sense that our approach is often haphazard. It doesn't leave room for manoeuvre to cope with unplanned events or to plan for future demands. This theme is about individual and team performance and defining the results you need.

Results management starts with understanding the context in which you are working by using a framework that considers a number of fundamental questions:

> **Each organisation is unique.**

- What are the major external influences on the organisation that create the context in which the results are to be managed?
- What are the internal organisational features and processes that impact on the role of the results manager?
- Is the role of the results manager universal to all organisational contexts?
- What are the benefits to you and the organisation of focusing on results management?

Next find out how to clearly identify the results you need to achieve. For instance, do you know how complex or risky the task is in relation to previous work you have undertaken? Do you know how to set about organising to deliver the required results and manage the associated risks? These questions are vital to your being a success at managing for results.

This theme looks at clarifying the results you need to achieve. You will:

- **Explore the internal and external influences that affect your role and responsibilities for supporting others to achieve results**
- **Use techniques to help clarify the task**
- **Reflect on your use of informal and formal approaches to managing for results.**

The context for managing results

The basic process for managing results involves the following steps:

- Clarifying the task and the required results
- Assessing the degree of complexity of the task in relation to previous tasks

- Identifying and securing the relevant resources, both people and facilities
- Agreeing how the task outcomes will be evaluated
- Clarifying your role as manager of the task and leader of the team
- Setting up and briefing the team
- Identifying areas of risk with the team and how to manage these
- Assessing the aspirations and motivation of individual team members.

This is a generic process that can be used on any task where teams are involved. Figure 1.1 shows the main elements.

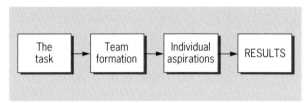

Figure 1.1 *The basic results management process*

Although the process is generic, it is likely that the context in which it takes place will vary enormously. Figure 1.2 shows the factors that affect this context. The success of the process depends on the skill and experience of the manager in diagnosing where the organisational context is likely to be a help or a hindrance. It is also important to recognise that organisations are not static and the factors that you identify will be in a constant state of change.

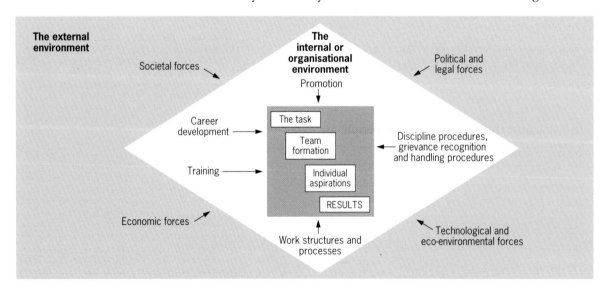

Figure 1.2 *The context for results management*

The external or industry environment

Organisations, and individuals working in them, are influenced by the state of the national economy, political and legal changes, technical and technological developments and societal values. A boost to contracts and investment in an industry will raise people's confidence in their future job prospects. A breakthrough in the technology that affects the working processes and products will encourage new thinking and enthusiasm towards the job. Where societal values are seen to be in tune with the activities of the organisation, then individuals will be much more prepared to raise their performance than where there is dissonance. Much of this may sound like the American 'motherhood and apple pie' message, but if you reflect on the impact of team performance in companies such as The Body Shop, Microsoft, leading children's and research hospitals, Shell Oil, Dyson Ltd, Planet Organic, Vodafone, Intel and many others, you can see the links at work.

You could do an Internet search to investigate the human resources policies of some of these organisations.

The internal or organisational environment

Each organisation is unique. Managers working in different organisations in the same industry, faced with similar tasks, find that working practices vary enormously. The underlying cause behind such differences can be attributed to differences in organisational culture. Organisational culture can be described as a cognitive or mental framework consisting of values, attitudes, behavioural norms and expectations that are shared by the majority of the workforce (Schein, 1985).

Here is how Chatman and Jehn (1994) characterise seven elements of organisational culture that can be used to describe an organisation.

Innovation: the degree to which people are expected to generate new ideas. The examples they give include MCI Communications where there are no procedure manuals so that staff can be encouraged to be unique. At 3M staff are given free time to develop their own ideas for new products.

Stability: valuing a rule-orientated work environment. They give examples from the Bank of America where only the safest investment advice is given to customers.

Orientation towards people: showing respect for individuals' rights; being fair and supportive.

Results-orientation: the extent of the concern and focus on achieving the desired results. Motorola, for example, is famous for its processes for reducing defects to zero.

Easygoingness: the extent to which the work atmosphere is relaxed and play is encouraged. They quote the case of Intel where the risk taking and camaraderie go hand in hand.

Attention to detail: the focus on analysis and precision. For example, at Merck, the prescription drug manufacturer, the view is that there is no room for error.

Collaborative orientation: here the attention is on working in teams. Companies such as 3M and Texas Instruments are seen as valuing teamwork as part of the research and product development process.

Being able to diagnose the organisational culture is a key step in understanding the context in which you are working. You must work within this culture to achieve the results you need. However, it is also important to understand how the operation of formal management processes impacts on the commitment of individuals and teams to the task. These processes have been designed to achieve conformity in standards of behaviour and should be understood and applied consistently. They are concerned with:

♦ training, career development and promotion

♦ work structuring, evaluation and control

♦ recognition and reward

♦ grievance recognition and handling, and discipline.

The skill is in knowing when the formal processes can be a positive help in achieving results and when a more informal or even original approach would be more effective.

Two examples of an informal approach to reward and recognition have been identified by Michael Rose and by Charles Handy:

Southwest Airlines has a sophisticated culture of recognition and celebration. It is reflected in the following guidelines:

♦ Say thank you often.

♦ Always celebrate people from the heart.

♦ Make heroes and heroines of employees who glorify your company's values.

♦ Find people who serve behind the scenes and celebrate their contributions.

♦ Celebrate at work the way you do at home.

♦ Celebrate at home the way you do at work.

In a 1999 pan-industry survey, 66% of managers said lack of recognition was the main factor that would make them leave their company. And a survey of 1,500 employees reported in *Industry Week* in 1995 found that the best motivator was to be personally congratulated by your manager.

Source: *Rose* (2000)

Charles Handy, in his book *The Elephant and the Flea* (2001), suggests that:

In the short term many large organisations are trying to buy the loyalty of key people with higher salaries. But there is a limit to how much money even the wealthiest organisation can throw at the problem. In time, they will have to rethink their reward strategies. For example SEMCO have 11 different methods of reward and a staff turnover of less than 1%.

Source: *Handy* (2001)

The benefits of results management

From the above you can see how important it is for achieving results to understand and harness the context in which the task is being executed. For you, as the person responsible for getting the task done and hence the results manager, the benefits are exactly the same as those sought by your team. These benefits are an opportunity to explore and release your motivation, learn how to direct your talents and energies in new ways, obtain satisfaction and recognition for a job well done, and to be an instrument in helping other people to do the same. On a tangible level there is the satisfaction that comes from executing the reward and responsibility contract that you have accepted from your employers. If everyone in the organisation focused on and practised results management, then the overall performance of the organisation would benefit and continue to provide exciting opportunities for employment and healthy personal growth.

Activity 1
Having an impact on results

Objectives

This activity will help you to:

♦ identify the key features in the external and internal organisational environment

♦ identify the key management processes in the organisation.

Task

1 What are the key features in the external environment and in the internal environment, and how do these impact on your efforts to deliver results? Note these features and their impact in the chart provided and prioritise them in terms of their impact.

	Key features and impact	*Priority*
External environment		
Internal environment		

2 What are the key formal management processes that are used in the organisation to help managers deliver results?

These include processes in areas such as:

Training and development

BOOK ORDER

WARRINGTON COLLEGIATE INST. 72700.001-001

Supplier	Dawson Books (UK)	Order Ref	00007
Order Date	15/11/2010 10:05:25	Item Ref	
Quantity	1	ISBN	9780080557465
Unit Price	28.99	Currency	GBP
Instructions			

Author	ELEARN		
Title	MANAGING FOR RESULTS		

Volume		Edition	
Format		Publisher	ELSEVIER SCIENCE & TECHNOLOGY
Shelf Mark		Date Publ.	08/09/2008
Site			
Fund			
Sequence			
Loan Type			
Quantity	1		

Work evaluation and control

Rewards and discipline

Grievances and disputes

You may wish to discuss your findings with a colleague.

Feedback

1 Did you find it difficult to see any connections between features in the external environment and your work? Often these features do have an impact, but because we feel that they are outside of our control, the tendency is to ignore them. Do you think it is correct to come to that conclusion?

   You probably found it much easier to identify features in the internal environment. Familiarity with the details of organisational life is a strength but can also be a weakness if we stop challenging barriers and constraints due to this familiarity.

2 Managers often ignore formal organisational processes or relegate them to the background, particularly when dealing with fast-changing situations. It helps to stand back to see ways in which you can make better use of these processes in managing for results. Remember that someone designed these procedures for the sole purpose of helping you to manage more effectively within the organisation. If they do not help, then you should seek ways to implement changes.

Clarifying the results that are required

For any task for which you accept responsibility for delivering results, it is essential to seek maximum clarification at the outset. Unfortunately, we always have to live with two major issues when working with others. First, there are uncertainties that surround the linkages between effort, actions and outcomes. Second, there are ambiguities that stem from our inability to capture the essence of the task and the problems that will unfold, and in the language we use. As we know, life is never a case of simply saying what results you require in order to get them. If it were, then life and work would be pretty dull.

Defining the task

So, we have to rely on our ability to be logical and draw on past experiences to help us define the task and the associated results that we must deliver. Best practice suggests that we aim to determine:

- a specific or series of objectives for the task that are clearly linked to the expectations of those involved
- the constraints on resources in terms of people, equipment and budget
- the time constraints
- the spread of skills and capacities among the resources and their match to the sub-tasks
- the degree of control which we have over the task and the degree that we need
- the responsibilities of the various parties that are involved and whether these have been recognised and accepted by those parties
- the risks involved in seeking to deliver the results, and how best to attempt to minimise those risks.

This process would be sufficient, if not easy to execute, for most of the tasks that we are likely to face. Tasks can be defined as well-structured, semi-structured or unstructured, but it is important to recognise that what one person might see as structured would be unstructured to another. When attempting to clarify a task, it is vital to take into account the personality of the person defining the task and the situation of the organisation. When a task is unstructured, you need to go further to define it more clearly.

Unstructured tasks

When tasks are unstructured, it is worth pursuing three distinct stages of definition:

Task analysis and redefinition, where there is a need to gather more information in order to begin the definition. This involves collating or refining a great deal of data and employing a degree of creativity in refining alternative definitions.

Idea generation, where the task definition is used to generate ideas and options about possible solutions. This involves opening up the thoughts and ideas held by the task setters.

Idea evaluation and choice, where the ideas are reduced to one or two that will be used to tackle the task. This can be an uncomfortable stage if the process involves confronting people about their ideas and can lead to conflict.

Alan Pearson (1991) has written extensively on managing in conditions of uncertainty and has provided some excellent examples of how organisations approach these situations. Reading these will help you when faced with the more unstructured task, where results are difficult to guarantee.

> Sony Corporation's Tape Recorder Division tried to redesign a small portable tape recorder so that it gave stereophonic sound. But they failed to reduce the size sufficiently and ended up with a prototype that couldn't record anything – but engineers used it to play their favourite music cassettes while they worked. Mr Ibuka, an honorary chairman, popped into the room, saw this and remembered a project that was developing lightweight portable headphones elsewhere in the building. The rest is history – the Walkman.

Source: *Nayak and Ketteringham* (1986)

> In the late 1940s Howard Head, an aerospace designer, metals expert and ski enthusiast, began to design, build and test metal skis. Despite disparaging comments from professionals he persuaded them to test them, and after three years of broken and twisted skis, he persisted, being described as 'possessed by his idea' and a 'fanatic'. He ran out of money and had to sell off 40 per cent of his company, and only after six to seven years and scores of design failures did he finally begin to make some money from his enterprise. Hundreds of others had tried to design metal skis but had failed. Head's skis worked so well they were called 'cheaters'. They sold for $100 in a market used to paying only $25 and helped to create the ski boom of the 1950s.

Source: *Quinn* (1986)

In trying to define a task, we are faced with uncertainties about the end outcomes or results and uncertainties about the means of getting there. Alan Pearson (1991) has given us what he calls the uncertainty map to help us decide on the optimum approach to adopt.

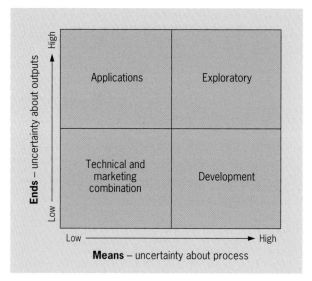

Figure 1.3 *The uncertainty map*   Source: *Pearson* (1991)

Figure 1.3 shows that where the form of the results is not clear and the means of doing the required work are not clear, then the approach to the task should be one of exploration, best tackled by a small team with minimum constraints and controls on their efforts. Where the anticipated results are clearer but the means of achieving them are not, then the approach should be one that emphasises development. This recognises that a lot of time and effort will be required before the results can be delivered. Where the uncertainty about the results is high but the means of tackling the work are well-established, the approach should be one that emphasises the application of existing work processes and skills. This is an approach that seeks a new product or service by using existing expertise. The final segment is where there is low uncertainty about the results and low uncertainty about the processes that are to be used: here we find tasks that combine both technical capability and market opportunity.

Matching team approaches to the task

As we have seen, not all tasks involve the same degree of complexity, uncertainty and ambiguity at the definition stage, and not all tasks benefit from a formal approach to managing the team's efforts.

Being aware of the need and place for these approaches is part of the skill of an effective results manager. Base your decision on a clear understanding of the context in which the task is being tackled and on the culture of the organisation.

Where the task involves the team working on predictable issues and problems that are easily defined and managed, then a formal management approach to the team's work will result in simple learning that reinforces existing beliefs and past experiences. This will be the case for most routine tasks. However, where the task is more complex, then the formal approach to managing the team will submerge the ambiguity. The team will find that the process itself encourages what is known as 'post-event rationalisation', particularly when the desired results are not achieved.

The informal team management approach tends to overcomplicate those tasks that are straightforward and the focus on achieving results will be lost. The informal approach, however, when used on ambiguous and complex tasks, encourages creativity and promotes new thinking to overcome blockages. But it will also create a team that threatens the status quo or accepted ways of working in the organisation. To get results when using this informal approach, your role changes from manager to that of visionary leader.

As a manager you need to develop your skills so that you are able to diagnose the level of complexity of the task and the risks associated with delivering the required results. From there you can determine how your skills and those of the team can best be applied within the organisational culture.

Activity 2
Setting up and managing tasks

Objectives

This activity will help you to:

◆ review your approach to setting up the task

◆ differentiate between structured and unstructured tasks

◆ reflect on your use of informal and formal approaches to managing for results.

Task

Reflect on your recent experiences of setting up and managing tasks. Then answer the following questions.

1 What steps do you follow when setting out to clarify the requirements of a new task? Having listed these steps, decide which are the ones that give you most difficulty and why this is so.

Steps you follow

2 Think of three recent tasks that you have undertaken where you had to deliver specific results, and list these in the chart provided. Which of these would you describe as unstructured and complex tasks and which were simple and well structured? Note your answer in the second column.

3 On reflection, did you adopt an informal or a formal approach to managing these tasks and do you feel that your approach was the most appropriate one in the circumstances? Record your ideas in the chart.

Task	Type	Informal/formal approach	Appropriate?

Feedback

For this activity to be of value, you need to have taken sufficient time to reflect on your approaches to recent tasks. As your management experience in delivering results increases, the tendency is to adopt a routine approach to tasks. Stepping back and reflecting on the extent to which the setting up and approach to managing tasks is being handled in an objective way will accelerate your learning. Too much reflection is as bad as too little and, as always, it is a question of finding the middle ground.

Most mistakes in managing for results occur at this setting up stage and taking time to check your approach will provide enormous returns.

◆ Recap

This theme has examined the organisational context for achieving results.

Explore the internal and external influences that affect your role and responsibilities for supporting others to achieve results

- ◆ The process for managing results involves looking at the task, the team formation, individual aspirations and the results required. This process has an impact on, and is impacted by, the internal and external environment.

- ◆ It is important to understand and harness the context in which the task is being executed to achieve results.

Use techniques to help clarify the task

- ◆ It is essential to seek maximum clarification at the outset of a task.

- ◆ Best practice indicates that we need to look at matching the tasks to individuals and to examine the constraints and skills available, the levels of control and responsibilities given to individuals and the risks involved.

- ◆ For unstructured tasks it is worth pursuing three distinct stages of definition: task analysis and definition; idea generation; idea evaluation and choice.

Reflect on your use of informal and formal approaches to managing for results

- ◆ As a manager you need to be able to develop your skills so that you are able to diagnose the level of complexity of the task and the associated risks.

- ◆ You can then use a formal or informal approach based on a clear understanding of the context and culture of the organisation.

▶▶ More @

Handy, C. (2001) *The Elephant and the Flea*, Hutchinson, Random House
Handy exchanged life in a corporation (the 'elephant' of his title) for the life of an independent (or 'flea'). In this book he explores the context of the organisation and where it is heading. 'Just as the signs were there 20 years ago for those who wished to see them, so I believe we can glimpse the shape of the new capitalist world even if it may take another 20 years to develop,' he writes. 'We may not like

what is coming but we would be foolish to think that we can plan our lives, or our children's lives, without giving some thought to the shape of the stage on which we and they will be strutting.' This text offers an interesting insight into the internal and external influences that might affect the way we work in the future.

Murdock, A. and Scutt, C. N. (2003) 3rd edition, *Personal Effectiveness*, Elsevier Butterworth-Heinemann
Personal Effectiveness introduces managers to the ideas, the underlying techniques and approaches required in terms of behaviour and skills to achieve effective performance. Chapter 4, Focus on Results, aims to help managers understand the impact of their behaviour on other people in a range of management situations. It covers goal setting and analysis, prioritising and using your time effectively.

www.findarticles.com
This is a useful online bank of articles – drawn from magazines and journals around the world. Try entering a search like 'managing for results'.

Full references are provided at the end of the book.

2   Motivation theory

Individual motivation is a key part of the results management process. This theme reviews human behaviour and motivation. It explores what is meant by motivation and looks briefly at why people work. It examines why motivation is important to organisations and managers who are working to achieve the organisation's goals.

Researchers and writers on the subject of motivation have taken different approaches and their theories can be classified under five main headings:

- needs hierarchy theory
- satisfiers and dissatisfiers
- expectancy theory
- goal-setting theory
- equity theory.

> **Motivation is probably the most complex and least understood aspect of organisational life.**

Here we look at each of these. These are classic theories that will provide insights to help you to support individuals and teams to complete the work they have been allocated.

This theme explores motivation theory. You will:

- **Explore the benefits of motivated employees in the workplace**
- **Explore the relevance of motivation theories to your role as a results manager**
- **Plan your personal goals and put your expectations into perspective**
- **Identify satisfiers and dissatisfiers within your job.**

The importance of motivation

Robertson et al. (1992) describe motivation as the psychological concept related to the strength and direction of human behaviour. It provides the driving force behind our actions and behaviour. Motivation, then, is the drive that leads individuals to take some action to achieve a goal that fulfils their needs or expectations. This idea of motivation is shown in Figure 2.1, which provides a basic motivational model.

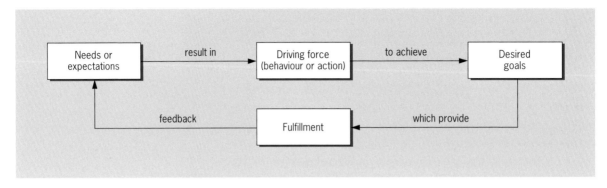

Figure 2.1 *Basic motivational model*   Source: *Mullins* (1999)

Why do people work?

The obvious answer is for money. Most people need to earn money to survive. But money isn't the whole story. Why is it that two people on the same income can have vast differences in their levels of motivation?

Numerous surveys have suggested that while money clearly has a role in motivating people to work, other factors come into play. One way analysts have explored this issue is to look at individuals' levels of job satisfaction.

Haygroup (2001) published some interesting research into the levels of job satisfaction experienced by committed workers and those of workers who were planning to leave their job. See Table 2.1.

Satisfaction with	Total % satisfied		Gap %
	Employees planning to stay for more than two years	Employees planning to leave in less than two years	
use of my skills and abilities	83	49	34
ability of top management	74	41	33
company has clear sense of direction	57	27	30
advancement opportunities	50	22	28
opportunity to learn new skills	66	38	28
coaching and counselling from one's own manager	54	26	28
pay	51	25	26
training	54	36	18

Table 2.1 *The relationship between job satisfaction and employee turnover*

Haygroup suggests the following:

Pay, usually considered the most emotional factor in the employer/employee relationship, is ranked seventh of the eight factors listed in Table 2.1. This will not surprise experienced managers, who know that although employees talk about money incessantly, it is not a deep motivator for most. Ultimately, people want to find meaning in their work. As our survey points out, meaning is generally derived from non-economic factors such as the desire to deploy one's own skills in a challenging effort – to be useful and helpful – and to play on a team led by capable managers who have a clear sense of direction.

You may want to look at Haygroup on its website –
www.haygroup.com

Source: *Haygroup* (2001)

Most social scientists and social psychologists would agree that people at work have a desire to make a good impression, to engage in interesting work and to be successful in achieving their goals. We recognise this as goal-directed behaviour. (You can see this in Figure 2.1). These desires create the drive behind a person's actions. People then adopt behaviours that enable them to satisfy those desires. However, motivation is also related to people's motives and the choices they make in deciding which behaviours to adopt. Depending on how well they judge themselves to have achieved their goals, they will either persist in those behaviours or adopt alternative behaviours.

The difficulty in determining these drives and behaviours, and people's willingness to maintain or abandon them, arises because they are held at a tacit or hidden level. We may not always fully understand why we behave the way we do. Also, identifying the drive that lies behind our actions does not always tell the whole story. For example, we know that people are still able to perform well at a task even when they are low on drive, and where they have little interest in the goals that have been set. On the other hand, someone who is highly motivated and recognises the value of the goal may well perform badly, perhaps due to lack of skills or poor management. We are also familiar with having many drives at the same time, some of which may be in direct conflict with each other.

The message here is that motivation is probably the most complex and least understood aspect of organisational life.

Simplistic notions, for example that people work for money and that people need to have interesting work in order to perform well, can be relegated to the bag labelled, 'Not wanted on this journey'. Managers have to seek a deeper understanding of what motivates their people if they are to build a motivated team that is committed to getting the results the organisation requires.

Benefits of motivated staff for organisations

Employees need the skills, knowledge and abilities to achieve the results required by organisations. They also need the will to achieve these results. The level of motivation among your team members is linked to their level of commitment to their work and their determination to do a good job. Mullins (1999) puts it succinctly:

Performance = motivation x ability

Measuring the contribution individuals make to an organisation's overall results is notoriously difficult. The combination of factors individuals contribute to an organisation is hard to quantify. However, research is beginning to show a clear link between employee satisfaction and company performance. For example, work carried out by Sears in the early 1990s suggested a direct link between employee satisfaction and performance (Rucci et al.1998). Linda Bilmes (2001), in an article drawn from her book *The People Factor*, explores the importance of people-management policies and their relationship to performance. She shows that research into companies in the United States and Germany found that companies committed to people management had high levels of employee satisfaction. It also found that companies which scored highest on a scorecard of people-management policies had a higher total shareholder return than lower-scoring companies.

We can also look at the experiences of individual companies.

Some benefits from the efforts of well-motivated teams in a range of organisations are as follows:

♦ Federal Express – reduced errors in incorrect bills, lost packages etc. by 13 per cent in 1989

♦ Corning – defects dropped from 1,800 parts per million to only 9 parts per million in its cellular ceramics plant

♦ Xerox – increased productivity by 30 per cent

♦ Eli Lilly – recorded the fastest ever roll-out time for a new medical product

♦ Exxon – achieved $10 million in savings in six months

♦ Sealed Air – waste reduced by 50 per cent and downtime cut from 20 per cent to 5 per cent in manufacturing plants

♦ Westinghouse Furniture Systems – found a 74 per cent productivity increase in three years.

Source: *Adapted from Wellins et al.* (1991), *Katzenbach and Smith* (1993) *and Osburn et al.* (1990)

What does motivation at work look like?

Table 2.2 lists just a few behavioural indicators of positive and negative motivation at work.

Positive indicators	Negative indicators
Arrives early for work	Has poor timekeeping
Volunteers for overtime – because of the workload	Has a higher than average level of sickness
Helps colleagues with their tasks	Has an apathetic approach
Takes responsibility	Is always grumbling
Provides support and encouragement to others	Avoids responsibility
Is willing to do extra work	Does the minimum
Is committed to achieving targets/goals	High error rate, increased waste
Communicates well with people	Complains about targets/goals or doesn't bother to achieve them
Asks constructive questions	
Is interested in developing self (and the team)	Always blames others, the system, etc. for faults, inadequacies
Works continually to improve self and job	Is not a team player
Enjoys work and the people	Endures work, couldn't care less about others
Is interested and concerned about the organisation, its future and his/her place in it	Considers quality is a waste of time
	Believes the organisation owes him/her a living

Table 2.2 *Indicators of motivation at work*

The columns in Table 2.2 show different ends of a motivational spectrum. From time to time, even well-motivated individuals may express or display negative behaviour, which could be related to work or other causes. However, you may like to consider how just small improvements in motivation levels among your staff could affect your results in terms of productivity, reduction in waste, better quality, lower absenteeism, satisfied customers ...

Key motivation theories

The first of the main theories of motivation explored here is Abraham Maslow's needs hierarchy theory.

Needs hierarchy

Abraham Maslow first published his work in 1943 (Maslow, 1987). His work is still relevant today. He developed a theory based on the assumption that behaviour is driven by needs. He says that whatever a person aspires to be, they must be – for example, a painter must paint, a musician must make music, a writer must write – and he refers to this need as 'self-actualisation'. However, before they get to this self-fulfilled (or self-actualised) stage of life or motivation, Maslow suggests that people have other needs which they must satisfy first. Only when they have satisfied these lower-order needs will people search for higher-order needs. He developed this theory into his hierarchy of needs, shown in Figure 2.2.

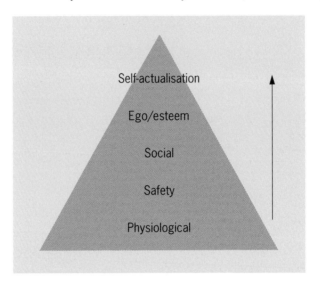

Figure 2.2 *Maslow's hierarchy of needs*   Source: *Maslow* (1987)

We'll look at each of these needs in turn.

Physiological needs. These are the things we need to maintain our bodies. They include the need for food, drink and shelter. Unless we are in reasonable working order, we probably aren't too worried about satisfying other needs. Obviously we can enjoy other facets of life if there are minor problems with our physiological state, but physiological needs override everything else.

Safety needs. If the physiological needs are generally satisfied, a new set of needs emerges. These safety needs may be characterised as protection from danger or deprivation, and include housing, a competent police service, heating, adequacy of food and water, and security from threats and harassment. In most societies, these needs are catered for by relatively stable government and by citizens operating within sets of laws, rules and regulations.

Social. If our physiological and safety needs are generally being met, we begin to think about our needs for love, friendship and belonging. Most people are predisposed to be loved, have friends and belong to a group or number of groups, such as a family group, social circle or sports/hobby group. Very often we do not understand our needs for love, friendship and belonging until we are deprived of them.

Ego/esteem. All people have a desire for a stable, high level of self-respect (or self-esteem) and also desire the esteem of others. Included in this category are reputation and status. Satisfaction of ego/esteem needs leads to feelings of self-confidence, self-worth, strength, capability, and of being useful and needed by others. If these ego/esteem needs are not satisfied, then feelings of inferiority, weakness and helplessness occur.

Self-actualisation. Having satisfied all lower-order needs, an individual can now realise their own potential for self-development and self-fulfilment in whichever way they choose. This self-development may be work related or could relate to any other aspect of personal or family life. In today's organisational context, companies are investing resources to help people become self-fulfilled within their careers – obviously to the benefit of their employers.

Maslow suggests that whatever level people are at or believe themselves to be at, if a lower-order need is unsatisfied, they are predisposed to satisfy it.

What does this all mean for you in your personal life and in your life as a manager? Consider whether Maslow's theory helps you to understand some aspects of human behaviour and motivation. Also, whether you can help people in your team to understand and manage their levels of need.

Satisfiers and dissatisfiers

An understanding of the links between the characteristics of tasks and motivation is important because it forms a basis for designing jobs that are both satisfying and motivating. Frederick Herzberg (1974) conducted research in the late 1950s which showed a relationship between job characteristics and human motivation. His research began by asking people about events that they had experienced at work which resulted either in a marked improvement in their job satisfaction or in a marked reduction in job satisfaction.

In Herzberg's view, the factors that create satisfaction – he calls these 'satisfiers' or 'motivators' – are those which stem from the **intrinsic** content of the job, for example the challenge, the complexity and the meaning of the job. These tend to satisfy individuals' higher needs. The factors that cause dissatisfaction – called 'dissatisfiers' or 'hygiene factors' – are those which stem from the **extrinsic** job content, for example pay, management and conditions of work. These tend to satisfy people's lower needs. Herzberg agrees with Maslow that people's higher needs are self-sustaining.

The key determinants of job satisfaction and job dissatisfaction identified by Herzberg are shown in Table 2.3.

Satisfiers	Dissatisfiers
Achievement	Company policy and administration
Recognition	Supervision
Work itself (job content)	Salary
The nature of tasks/goals/objectives	Interpersonal relations
Responsibility	Working conditions
Advancement	

Table 2.3 *Determinants of satisfaction and dissatisfaction*

An interesting aspect of Herzberg's research is that the gratification of a lower need does not produce satisfaction, it merely eradicates dissatisfaction. In other words, if the organisation attends to the extrinsic job factors it will minimise dissatisfaction, but this in itself will not create motivation.

A good example of this dissatisfaction was in car parking arrangements at a large company in the north of England.

There were very few parking places outside the main buildings and they were reserved for directors and some senior managers. All other managers and staff had to walk several hundred yards from the main car park to and from work. Much dissatisfaction was felt by staff who couldn't park close to work. They resented what they felt to be the smug grins of the senior managers who drove past them into their reserved parking area – especially in winter months. A new chief executive officer (CEO) barred all directors and senior managers from the parking places outside the building, and said that it was now reserved for customers and visitors. The source of dissatisfaction disappeared overnight for 95 per cent of the staff. The CEO was immediately popular and he always chatted with staff on his walk to and from the main car park where no spaces were reserved. (Note that this was just one change in a radical overhaul of the company.)

Your role as manager is to ensure that people derive as much satisfaction as possible from the work they do, and that the extrinsic factors do not detract from their overall job satisfaction. Much unrest and discontent among staff can arise from factors which have nothing to do with their work – as in the car park example.

Expectancy theory

Theorists are agreed that there is no one best way to motivate people. There are too many variables among the people and the situations involved. A theory that takes account of these variables is expectancy theory. Vroom described his model in 1964 and this was developed by Porter and Lawler (1968) when they linked expectations and performance. It works on the principle that people are influenced by the expected results of their actions and prefer certain outcomes from their behaviour over others. Mullins (1999) gives a good example of different forms of expectation:

> The desire for promotion will result in higher performance if the person believes there is a strong expectation that this will lead to promotion. But on the other hand, if the person believes that promotion is a result of age, length of service, length in the job etc., there is no motivation to achieve a high level of performance.

Source: *Mullins* (1999)

Robertson et al. (1992) point out that effort and performance are not always related. They cite the example of someone who practises with a musical instrument for hours on end – they might never be a concert performer, but they should develop some capability to play the instrument. If we take this point into the workplace, you may have to deal with an individual who has worked extremely hard, but their efforts have not delivered what was required. How you deal with this individual may influence their future commitment and will affect your relationship.

Another element of expectancy theory is 'instrumentality'. This relates to what the performance, once achieved, will pay off in terms of outcomes. If we link expectancy and instrumentality in a work situation it might look something like this:

> A sales executive agrees to make contact with 25 potential new clients within six months. He believes that, given the effort, it should be possible to contact 25 people (expectancy) but for the effort to be worthwhile he must also believe that a proportion of the new contacts, say 15, will produce the desired level of outcomes – conversion of contacts to new business (instrumentality).

There are two levels of outcomes, first and second level. First level is what you achieve as a direct result of performance (in our example, 25 new contacts with 15 converting to sales). The second level outcome is what you achieve as a result of selling to 15 new clients (satisfaction, recognition, reward, etc.). This is illustrated in Figure 2.3.

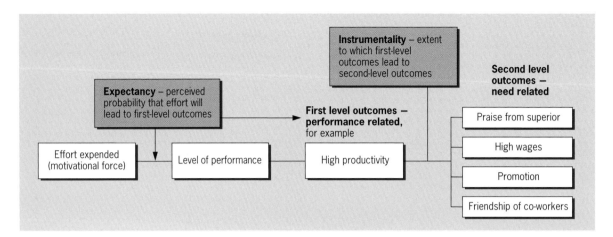

Figure 2.3 *Basic model of expectancy theory*   Source: *Mullins* (1999)

The final element of expectancy theory is 'valence' – the extent to which possible outcomes are attractive for the individual concerned. It is different from 'value' which is the actual satisfaction provided by the outcome. So, if expectancy and valence are both high, then motivational behaviour should result. But if expectancy and valence are low, then little or no motivation will result.

> In our sales executive example, if he agrees to make five new contacts, valence may be low because he perceives the target lacks challenge and would not really be worth his effort. Similarly, if he agrees to make 40 new contacts, he might regret this later when he realises it is too high, and consequently will not be motivated towards achieving it.

In managing your team, you should determine what particular outcomes or rewards are valued by each individual and be specific about the precise behaviours that constitute good levels of performance.

Goal-setting theory

Like expectancy theory, many psychologists have been involved in the development of goal-setting theory, but the original work is attributed to Locke, who first published his theory on the effect of goal setting on performance in 1968 (see Locke and Latham, 1990). Locke suggests that provided a goal relates to the performance criteria used and it is accepted by the individual, then measurement criteria can be introduced to determine whether (and how well) the individual's performance matches the goal. This is illustrated in Figure 2.4.

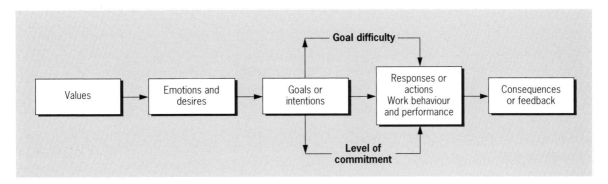

Figure 2.4 *Locke's theory of goal setting*   Source: *Mullins* (1999)

Another facet of goal setting is that the nature of the goal determines the effort expended in achieving it. Locke and Latham (1990) say that people who have agreed specific, difficult (stretching) goals will perform better than people with easy goals or none at all. However, it is important to note that people will work towards achieving difficult goals only if they are committed to them and perceive them to be achievable.

You should always involve your staff in goal setting wherever possible, but if you are given goals that you need to distribute among your team, then you will need to convince them of the need for the goals before they will be fully committed to achieving them.

Equity theory

Equity theory was first introduced by Adams (1965). It is concerned with people's individual perceptions of how fairly they have been treated, compared with the treatment that other people received. Adams argues that people compare themselves on two variables: outcomes and inputs. Outcomes are associated with things such as pay, fringe benefits and prestige, whereas inputs refer to the contribution that the person has made, particularly with respect to time worked and effort expended on the job.

The main point is that people make the comparison between outcomes and inputs based on their own perceptions rather than on any objective measurements or standards. If they feel that the ratio of outcomes to inputs is greater or less than that of other people, there is a feeling of inequity. This subjective perception leads to a lot of disagreement on what constitutes equitable treatment in the job.

Adams saw that if people consider that they are in a state of overpayment inequity, they experience associated feelings of guilt when they compare themselves with other people. Alternatively, if they consider that they are in a state of underpayment inequity, their comparison with others leads to feelings of anger. These feelings of anger and guilt are unpleasant and people take some action to minimise feelings of tension. For example, if you experience overpayment inequity, your response may be to rationalise that you work harder than others do and thus deserve greater rewards. On the other hand, if you experience underpayment inequity, you may convince yourself that the other workers are more qualified and so deserve a greater reward. Alternatively, you may alter your inputs or seek to alter your outcomes, or pressurise others to alter theirs, in order to create greater equity.

It is the ability to change the way that people see things and hence the impact it has on performance and striving for results that makes this theory relevant to your work.

The activities that follow illustrate how Maslow's and Herzberg's theories can be applied to help you reflect on different aspects of your life.

Activity 3
Maslow's hierarchy of needs

Objectives

This activity will help you to:

- reflect on different aspects of your life and what is important to you
- put your personal goals and ambitions into perspective.

Maslow's hierarchy of needs is shown in Figure 2.5.

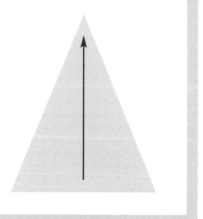

5 Self-actualisation

4 Ego/esteem

3 Social

2 Safety

1 Physiological

Figure 2.5 *Maslow's hierarchy of needs*   Source: *Maslow* (1987)

Task

To put your goals and ambitions into perspective, reflect on those elements within your life which you consider to be important, for example job, career, family, relationships, hobbies, interests, etc.

1   Using Maslow's hierarchy of needs, determine which areas of your
    life are at levels 3, 4 and 5 and why you believe this to be so.

Area of life	Why you believe it to be so
Level 3	
Level 4	
Level 5	

2   Consider those areas of your life that you believe to be in levels 3
    and 4 – do you need to improve them? If so, what might you do to
    improve them?

Improvements you might make:

You may wish to discuss this activity with your partner, a close friend
or a colleague.

Feedback

So, how are you with your life – do you know the areas in which you are content and areas in which you have not yet self-actualised (your ambitions)? Were you clear about these areas before you carried out this activity?

We should all have goals and ambitions, but in undertaking this activity you should be careful to separate these from wishes. Goals are realistic because we work towards achieving them. Wishes are just that, but they can become goals with energy, commitment and tangible efforts to work towards their achievement.

An example is a man who is reasonably successful across most areas of his life, such as education, job, family, social life. However, his real passion is playing the piano. He has spent a lot of his spare time practising and he now plays to a very high standard. He has an unrealised ambition to play in public, but isn't sure how to make this happen. In discussion with his wife, she suggests he play at a forthcoming local charity concert in which she is involved. This means that, in terms of his music, he will self-actualise (level 5). He and his wife would like to have children, but as they have not yet done so they have an unsatisfied social need (level 3).

Activity 4
Herzberg's satisfiers and dissatisfiers

Objective

This activity will help you to identify satisfiers and dissatisfiers within your job.

Task

This is an excellent activity to share with your team to determine what is helping and hindering effective performance. You can do this activity either in focus groups or by copying it and handing it to colleagues. The best results will be given if people complete the activity independently.

1   What is it about the intrinsic and extrinsic elements of your job that satisfy and dissatisfy you? List your responses in the chart provided and show whether:

  ◆ they are personal to you (P)

  ◆ you believe they also affect other members of your team (T).

Intrinsic satisfiers	P	T	Intrinsic dissatisfiers	P	T
	☐	☐		☐	☐
	☐	☐		☐	☐
	☐	☐		☐	☐
	☐	☐		☐	☐

Extrinsic satisfiers (hygiene factors)	P	T	Extrinsic dissatisfiers (hygiene factors)	P	T
	☐	☐		☐	☐
	☐	☐		☐	☐
	☐	☐		☐	☐
	☐	☐		☐	☐

2   What can you and your team do to influence or overcome areas of dissatisfaction?

List these below and discuss them with your team and your own managers:

◆   ◆

◆   ◆

◆   ◆

◆   ◆

Feedback

Your own and your team's responses should give you a good insight into activities that are both satisfying and dissatisfying. Are there any surprises between your responses and theirs? Remember that people view their workplace differently and therefore a range of responses will emerge. However, you are looking for similarities that will enable you to promote the common satisfiers and work to eradicate the dissatisfiers.

For this activity to be meaningful, it is important that it does not descend into a whinging session about some personal/ organisational issues. Comments should be constructive.

You may wish to discuss your findings with other managers, including your own and the human resources manager, especially if some dissatisfiers are outside your area of responsibility.

◆ Recap

Motivation theories can be used as a framework to examine our own actions and behaviours and those of others around us.

Explore the benefits of motivated employees in the workplace

- Motivation provides the driving force behind our actions and behaviour. Performance = motivation × ability.

- Research suggests that there is a clear link between job satisfaction, motivation and organisational performance.

Explore the relevance of motivation theories to your role as a results manager

- Researchers have taken a number of approaches to the subject of motivation.

- There are five leading theories of motivation relevant to your own role:
  - needs hierarchy theory
  - satisfiers and dissatisfiers
  - expectancy theory
  - goal-setting theory
  - equity theory.

Plan your personal goals and put your expectations into perspective

- Maslow's hierarchy of needs is presented to help you structure your reflections on your goals and ambitions in your personal, social and professional life.

Identify satisfiers and dissatisfiers within your job

- Here you explored the links between the characteristics of tasks and motivation.

- You also identified how both satisfiers and dissatisfiers affect your motivation and that of your team.

▶▶ More @

Katzenbach, J. R. and Smith, D. K. (1998) *The Wisdom of Teams*, **McGraw-Hill**
This book looks at what differentiates various levels of team performance, where and how teams work best, and how to enhance their effectiveness. *The Wisdom of Teams* includes stories and case examples involving real people and situations and shows why teams will be the primary building blocks of organisational performance in the future. Commitment to performance goals and common purpose is more important to team success than team building.

Maslow, A. H. (1987) 3rd edition, *Motivation and Personality*, **Harper and Row**
This is a classic text which defines self-actualisation and describes the data which contributed to the theory. Applications are made to the theories and science of personality, psychotherapy, personal growth and general psychology.

Stredwick, J. (2000) *An Introduction to Human Resource Management*, **Elsevier Butterworth-Heinemann**
A comprehensive and wide-ranging text that examines all the major aspects of human resource management in a down-to-earth and practical way. Chapter 6 focuses on effective ways of working and in particular on motivation theories.

Thomson, R. (2002) 3rd edition, *Managing People*, **Elsevier Butterworth-Heinemann**
Managing People addresses the perspective of the individual manager whose role includes the management of people, as well as issues concerning the organisation as a whole. See particularly Chapter 5 'Motivation, job satisfaction and job design'.

Tyson, S. and York, A (2000) 4th edition, *Essentials of HRM*, **Elsevier Butterworth-Heinemann**
The Essentials of HRM combines an overview of organisational behaviour with a detailed explanation of human resources management policies and techniques. It also acts as an introduction to the study of industrial relations. The first section of the book examines behaviour in organisations, including motivation and managerial theories.

Wellins, R. S., Byham, W. C. and Wilson, J. M. (1991) *Empowered Teams*, **Jossey-Bass**
This book provides answers to questions about how teams work, what makes them effective, when they are useful, how to get them going and how to maintain their vigour and productivity in the long run.

Haygroup www.haygroup.com
This website contains a number of articles and resources about human resource issues. Click on the 'research library' button to search the resources.

Full references are provided at the end of the book.

3   Motivation to achieve results

This theme looks at some of the practicalities of motivating to achieve results. We look at how managers and organisations encourage team participation and explore some work factors that motivate people. You will be able to benchmark your own team against the characteristics of high performing teams.

The working environment and conditions have a direct impact on staff motivation and productivity. Consider the aspects that you can influence or modify and those you cannot. You will also need to review your responsibilities for ensuring fairness and open communications with people within your areas of responsibility.

Rewards are one of the key motivators for people to work. There are different ways in which an organisation and a manager can reward people for their contributions and effort. These include non-monetary rewards, informal rewards, team rewards and rewards linked to results.

This theme illustrates techniques you can use to motivate your team. You will:

♦ **Use techniques to help you identify and understand the causes of motivation and demotivation**

♦ **Benchmark your team's performance against some characteristics of high-performing teams**

♦ **Identify the scope of your responsibilities for working conditions**

♦ **Understand the range of formal and informal rewards available to you for use with your team.**

Motivation in practice

Motivation theory shows that a person's motivation comes from within – it involves our feelings, needs and drives – and what motivates one person may leave another totally unmoved.

Can a manager motivate?

What part can a manager play in motivating staff? Kathy Schofield, Director of Human Resources at HFC Bank, puts it neatly:

> You don't motivate individuals. You provide them with an environment to be self-motivated. It is a personal decision, but it's management's job to provide the right environment.

Source: *Cited in Crainer* (1995)

People can be very different in their personal motivations and behaviours, and harnessing all of these differences towards the common goal is not easy to achieve. Your role as the manager is to provide the conditions in which staff motivation can be directed towards:

♦ the organisation's goals and the results you are required to achieve

♦ their individual tasks

♦ the people with whom they interact.

In order to provide the right environment and encourage individuals to be motivated in their work, you have to get to know your people on a personal level. What are they looking for from their work? Which of Maslow's needs are important to them at work? You also have to establish clear work objectives and clear outcomes. Be clear about what the results will be when the team achieves its targets, and be consistent so that there is a clear link between expectations and performance. To consider what action you can take to improve the environment to enable people to be motivated, it is helpful to differentiate between intrinsic and extrinsic motivational factors at work.

Intrinsic and extrinsic motivational factors

Herzberg's work on motivation highlighted the differences between extrinsic and intrinsic factors. Extrinsic factors relate to the elements that surround the job, but which are not directly involved in doing the job. They include:

♦ the potential of the job – what the job offers the individual in terms of potential for wider/higher employment

♦ rewards – salary and other benefits including non-financial benefits

♦ employment security

♦ working conditions – physical and psychological

♦ the status of the job – both within the organisation and beyond

♦ relationships with team leader/manager and co-workers

♦ opportunities for self-development

♦ satisfaction with organisational and management cultures.

Extrinsic factors play an important role in contributing to a person's overall satisfaction level. As Herzberg suggests, satisfaction with a job does not foster motivation in a person, but it is a necessary condition for motivation to take place. If these factors are not addressed by management, they can have a marked effect on both an individual's and a group's level of motivation and ultimately their performance.

Intrinsic factors are related to the job itself or how the person feels about the job, and include:

- what the job is about, and whether it stimulates the individual
- the variety of work within the job
- where the job fits within the team
- the identity of the job – whether it is visible and recognised positively by others
- the importance or significance of the job to the organisation
- the clarity of goals or objectives, and whether these are agreed and are challenging, yet realistic
- the autonomy to undertake the job in a manner that suits the individual as well as the organisation
- the ability to create, innovate, recommend changes or improvements
- the level of responsibility – whether it is appropriate for the job.

According to Herzberg, it is these intrinsic aspects of a job that can help to increase individual levels of motivation. Therefore, the design of a job is important, and we will look at this next.

Job design

Job design is about the relationship between the content and characteristics of a job and the people doing the job. It involves seeking to meet the needs of individuals at work by reorganising or restructuring the job.

Job enlargement involves expanding a job by increasing its scope and the range of tasks. Although it gives a person more to do and may increase variety, it will not help to provide a sense of achievement if it simply involves doing more boring, routine tasks. If you use job enlargement, you should be sure that the added responsibilities could be undertaken by an average person in that job, otherwise it may be difficult to justify enlarging the job. Job enlargement is often disliked – employees may see it as the organisation trying to get more work out of fewer staff – and you may find that it does nothing to motivate people.

Job enrichment is used to make a job more interesting. It usually involves giving people more responsibility and greater involvement in the planning and control of their work. Mullins (1999) suggests that jobs can be enriched by:

◆ giving people greater control over the planning of their work

◆ giving people a complete task to do, rather than part of it

◆ giving people tasks that challenge their abilities and make full use of their skills, expertise and training

◆ giving people the opportunities to have greater direct contact with their internal and external customers

◆ promoting self-managed teams, where the team members themselves take responsibility for monitoring their own performance.

Hackman and Oldham (1980) developed a model of job enrichment, which has become well known. This is illustrated in Figure 3.1.

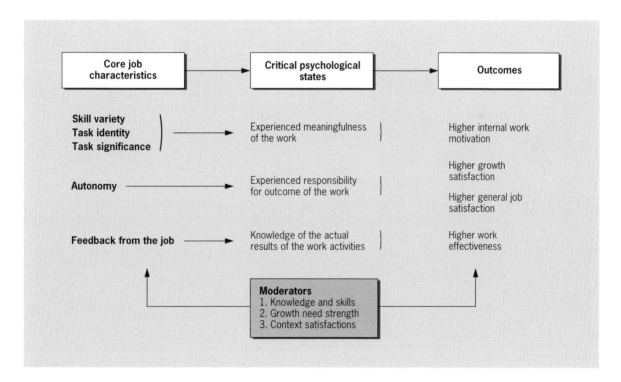

Figure 3.1 *A model of job enrichment*

Source: *Hackman and Oldham* (1980)

This model suggests that by attending to five core characteristics of a job, you can improve the psychological state experienced by doing the work, and this in turn will lead to outcomes that include greater job satisfaction and work motivation. The moderators are the factors that will affect the scope there is for enriching the job. The first two moderators are self-evident, but we can take 'context satisfactions' to mean aspects of the work environment, such as working conditions, sociability and so on, which contribute to satisfaction or otherwise with the job.

The five core characteristics in more detail are:

- ◆ skill variety – the range of skills and activities required to do the job

- ◆ task identity – whether the task has a clear outcome (or whether it is only part of a whole)

- ◆ task significance – its impact on other people

- ◆ autonomy – the independence and discretion to plan the work and decide how best to do it

- ◆ feedback from the job – whether information on performance is provided.

Teamworking

One method of job enrichment suggested above is teamworking. Katzenbach and Smith (1993) define a team as:

...a small number of people with complementary skills who are committed to a common purpose, performance goals and approach, for which they hold themselves mutually accountable.

Source: *Katzenbach and Smith* (1993)

In this definition, teamworking is likely to encourage team members to be motivated, but organisations set up different leadership or management structures for teams. At one end of the spectrum is a basic work team with the manager or team leader controlling and directing the work. At the other end is the self-managed team, where the members themselves have autonomy in their decision making and planning, and the manager is outside the team in the role of facilitator. This is illustrated in Figure 3.2.

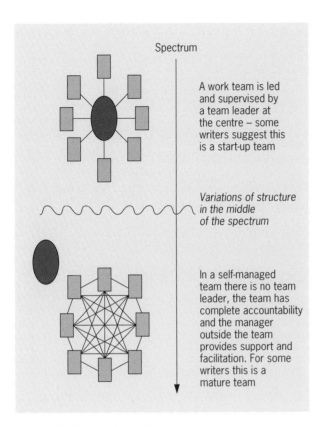

Spectrum

A work team is led and supervised by a team leader at the centre – some writers suggest this is a start-up team

Variations of structure in the middle of the spectrum

In a self-managed team there is no team leader, the team has complete accountability and the manager outside the team provides support and facilitation. For some writers this is a mature team

Figure 3.2 *Leadership in teams*

The idea of self-managed teams is based on the efforts of social scientists to integrate people with the technical environment in which they are working. Technical advancement means that a few, highly skilled people can now undertake work which previously needed to be done by many people. Furthermore, the nature of work has changed. Computers now manage many mundane but essential processes with much better quality outputs and standardisation than could be achieved by people. An example is a car assembly line, which is highly automated, with robots undertaking much or all of the work on the line. People are responsible for controlling, monitoring and maintaining the robots, to ensure that the components reach the right area of the line at the right time. The cultural or social make-up of the organisation has to be right for self-managed teams to operate and prosper. Mullins (1999) provides the following key features of self-managed workgroups:

♦ Specific goals are set for the team; team members decide how these goals will best be met

♦ Team members have greater freedom and choice, and wider discretion over planning, execution and control of their work

♦ Team members possess the collective variety of expertise and skills to successfully undertake tasks

> ◆ The level of external supervision is reduced and the role of supervisor is more one of giving advice and support to the team
>
> ◆ Feedback and evaluation are related to the performance of the team as a whole.

Source: *Mullins* (1999)

For more about self-managed teams you could check out: Manz and Sims (1993) Business without Bosses *or Katzenbach and Smith (1993)* The Wisdom of Teams.

Motivational characteristics of high-performing teams

The best way of describing a well-motivated team is to suggest that the outcomes it produces are synergistic – the output is greater than the sum of the parts. For example, a cohesive team of less-gifted footballers may beat a 'team' of superstars who are individually gifted but not playing together as a team.

A great deal of research has been undertaken over many years into the characteristics of high-performing teams. Here are a few examples of the motivators of such teams:

Respect – for each other, including individual contributions and individual areas of expertise. Also respect for the rights of the individual and of the team to voice different views. Remember that you do not have to like someone to respect them. Respect involves accepting a person's right to their individuality, and acknowledging that differences can be enhancing rather than threatening.

Trust – the confidence that all team members can be relied upon to do what is expected of them, and to contribute individual and team effort towards goal achievement.

Commitment – the understanding that each member of the team is committed to their own, other people's and team goals and objectives. Also that they will willingly add their contributions to ensure these are achieved.

Understanding – the knowledge that all members of the team have personal and work needs, both inside and outside the team, and that these needs have to be understood and addressed so as not to detract from overall individual and team performance. This understanding builds into a rapport among the team members.

Communications – open, frequent and honest communication among the team members, and between the team and the wider organisation. Very often people do not say what they feel or what they believe because the team situation is not conducive to openness. In such situations, people talk among themselves and an individual's negative perceptions may quickly become the team reality – without any clear foundation. This is clearly detrimental to individual and team motivation. Responsibility for open communications lies with all team members, but as a manager you can promote good communications.

Clear goals/objectives – people like to know what is expected of them, and how their effort fits into the team and the wider organisational goals. If they understand exactly what is required of them, people generally display more commitment to task/goal achievement.

Problem solving and decision making – this includes the degree of autonomy and scope given to the team. The greater the autonomy, the more committed people are likely to be to overcoming problems. If problems arise within a job or within a team, people should be encouraged to help resolve these problems and contribute to the decision-making process.

Enjoyment of work – if people are happy at work they will be more motivated to perform their jobs and to help other team members. Enjoyment arises from a complex set of personal and organisational criteria that blend to produce a stimulating environment. Of course, just because one person really enjoys everything that is happening at work, this is not necessarily the case for other team members.

Leadership – the style of leadership and the team's feelings and perceptions about their leader, and vice versa, relate directly to the level of motivation within the team. Leaders should seek to build a good level of understanding and rapport, which involves respect, trust, commitment and understanding, all wrapped up in ongoing, effective two-way communications. This should result in a good level of motivation within the team to support you in meeting your goals or objectives.

The activities that follow will help you to: assess motivation levels in your team; understand the causes of motivation and demotivation; benchmark your team's performance against some characteristics of high-performing teams.

Activity 5
Motivation in the workplace

Objective

This activity will help you to assess the level of staff motivation within your area of responsibility.

Task

Answer the questions in the table to form your view of motivation in your workplace.

How would you describe the level of motivation:	Poor	Average	Good	High
1 Across the organisation at your work location?	☐	☐	☐	☐
2 Within your work division or department?	☐	☐	☐	☐
3 Within your work team?	☐	☐	☐	☐
4 Within yourself – in relation to work?	☐	☐	☐	☐
5 Are your responses consistent?	Yes ☐	No ☐		

Remember, we cannot measure motivation as it is intangible, but it should be possible to observe the effects of motivation. What is it that you see, read, hear and experience that makes you arrive at these conclusions?

Is there scope for improvement at any of the three organisational levels and within yourself? If so, what can you do or influence to bring about improvements?

You may wish to undertake this activity in conjunction with other members of your team and share your findings with them.

What I can do to improve matters:	What I can influence (e.g. through discussions with your boss or other managers):

Feedback

The level of team and individual member motivation has a direct impact on commitment, productivity, quality, timekeeping, attendance, sickness, etc.

It is particularly important that you act on matters that are demotivating the team. You should work to eradicate these and, if necessary, discuss them with your boss.

Activity 6
The meaning of motivation

Objective

This activity will help you to identify and understand causes that motivate and demotivate people.

Case study

Read the case study before you complete the task.

Peter has recently taken over as team leader in a new appointment and he is already experiencing problems with one of his staff, Colin, who is a very difficult man to deal with. It seems that Colin is never satisfied, everyone is always wrong and he is always right. These issues cause particular problems with other members of the team who don't like or respect him and avoid him as much as possible.

Colin's output has a higher error rate than that of the other members of the team which also causes problems for the people who receive his work – their productivity is also suffering. Colin often arrives late and he has a higher than average sickness record, but he always has an excuse which places the blame for his absence on other people or issues, for example, the bus was late! Peter has to spend a lot of time monitoring Colin's work which means that he has less time to spend with better performing team members who he knows he should be developing.

Over lunch with another team leader, Peter was discussing his problems with Colin. The other team leader was really surprised as he knows Colin socially. He told Peter that Colin is a respected, popular and valued member of the local drama group where he is the secretary and treasurer. In addition, whenever a production is forthcoming, Colin works long hours in the evenings and at weekends building stage scenery and he is regarded as the main driving force in the overall success of the drama group. Peter wondered if he and his fellow team leader were talking about the same person!

Task

Put yourself in Peter's position and note below the issues that you consider to be impacting on Colin's performance and the actions you should take before meeting with Colin to discuss his poor performance and negative demeanour.

Issues impacting on Colin's performance:	Actions I should take:

Feedback

Here are some points to consider. The big surprise for Peter is not that Colin is difficult or producing poor work, but that he is such a pillar of society outside work. The chat with the other team leader gave Peter some clues as to the issues he should address before meeting with Colin to discuss his poor performance and negative demeanour. He started thinking about the situation:

♦ Colin is obviously much happier in one aspect of his personal life than at work.

♦ All of the incidents at work are symptomatic of someone who doesn't care or is very unhappy, or both.

♦ Lack of motivation towards the work, the team/manager/ organisation, etc. may be caused by either intrinsic or extrinsic dissatisfiers.

♦ The poor performance may be the effect of a cause which is not work related, but Colin appears to be putting his heart and soul into his drama club – no apparent dissatisfiers there.

♦ Peter doesn't know anything about Colin's home life – might his deep involvement with the drama club hide problems at home?

♦ Peter would make subtle enquiries about Colin's home life.

♦ Peter needs to understand Colin's background and past performance at work, and would review his personal file and previous performance record with the human resources manager before meeting Colin.

♦ Peter would contact Colin's previous boss to ask him for any background information which might help his understanding of the situation.

♦ Peter does not want to implement disciplinary action if it is inappropriate – he might just be dealing with the effect and not addressing the cause.

♦ Peter would consider whether Colin's demeanour and poor performance might be related to stress or other illness. He made a mental note to discuss this with the HR manager as well.

Most people want to produce good work and be well regarded by their colleagues. If people underperform, there are often good reasons for this which may be connected to the workplace and may be the effect of other (external) causes. You should do everything possible to identify and understand the causes by encouraging the individual to talk about their work and other aspects of their life. If you just deal with the effects, you may do no more than 'paper over the cracks' and subsequent, more serious lapses may occur.

Activity 7
Team motivational and performance survey

Objectives

This activity will help you to:

◆ benchmark your team's performance against some characteristics of high-performing teams

◆ consider and implement improvements.

Task

This survey asks you to reflect on and comment on your team's level of motivation and, in doing so, gauge your team's overall level of performance. The survey is about team-based issues and behaviours within and amongst the team members. Include your manager or team leader as an integral member of the team. We have included one extra topic that was not included in the text, 'Relationships at work', which we believe needs to be separated from the work-based issues of enjoyment at work.

This activity will be more powerful if you give copies to each member of your team and arrive at an overall team rating as well as individual ratings.

In scoring your responses, be as honest and objective as possible. If there are areas that need improvement, you won't be doing yourself or the team any favours by over-scoring.

Scoring:

6	Outstanding	3	Just satisfactory
5	Very good	2	Unsatisfactory
4	Good	1	Poor

The descriptions in the middle column represent an ideal situation – score 6. You have to decide how well your team matches the ideal scores.

Motivational and performance characteristics		*Score for your team*
Respect	People respect each other, their capabilities and their strengths and weaknesses. The team respects people's individuality and their right to voice different views. Difference is regarded as enhancing rather than threatening	☐ ☐ ☐ ☐ ☐ ☐ 1　2　3　4　5　6
Trust	Individuals can be relied upon to do what is expected of them and they are trusted to contribute willingly towards overall team achievement	☐ ☐ ☐ ☐ ☐ ☐ 1　2　3　4　5　6
Commitment	People are committed towards their individual and team goals – they willingly help each other	☐ ☐ ☐ ☐ ☐ ☐ 1　2　3　4　5　6
Understanding	There is a high level of rapport and understanding throughout the team, incorporating people's personal and work needs	☐ ☐ ☐ ☐ ☐ ☐ 1　2　3　4　5　6
Communications	Open, regular and effective communications are practised throughout the team and beyond the team with suppliers and customers. Team members always know what is happening in and around the team	☐ ☐ ☐ ☐ ☐ ☐ 1　2　3　4　5　6
Clear goals/ objectives	Every member of the team knows what is expected of them and how their job fits into the bigger picture. Everyone has clear individual goals, linked to team goals that are clearly aligned with higher goals	☐ ☐ ☐ ☐ ☐ ☐ 1　2　3　4　5　6
Problem solving and decision making	The team enjoys a high level of involvement in problem solving and decision making across a wide range of issues which affect it, together with the autonomy to implement decisions	☐ ☐ ☐ ☐ ☐ ☐ 1　2　3　4　5　6
Enjoyment of work	The work is challenging, stimulating and has sufficient variety to stop people from becoming bored	☐ ☐ ☐ ☐ ☐ ☐ 1　2　3　4　5　6
Relationships at work	Relationships amongst the team members and between the team, their suppliers and customers are excellent	☐ ☐ ☐ ☐ ☐ ☐ 1　2　3　4　5　6
Leadership	The leadership approach is democratic and enables the team to function as an integrated unit within defined limits	☐ ☐ ☐ ☐ ☐ ☐ 1　2　3　4　5　6

Total

Feedback

What do the scores tell you? Compare your own scores and the team consensus result against our chart.

51–60	Outstanding	Motivation is excellent across the team with no discernible areas of weakness. This is a high-performing team. Customers and suppliers will enjoy dealing with your team
41–50	Very good	You are a member of an effective team with identifiable weaknesses in some areas. By addressing these areas your team should soon be a more highly motivated and high-performing team. Your customers and suppliers will be highly satisfied with your outputs
31–40	Good	Your team is well motivated in some areas, but there are other areas which need attention. Swift actions are needed to ensure your team does not lose any more effectiveness. Customers and suppliers are pleased with your outputs, but there is room for improvement
21–30	Just satisfactory	The team is not performing well. Motivation is a problem in some areas and actions are needed to rectify the situation. Performance will not improve until motivation is addressed. You will receive some complaints from customers/suppliers
11–20	Unsatisfactory	Motivation is a major problem within this team. There are significant shortfalls across several areas which need to be addressed urgently. Performance is well below acceptable levels. Complaint levels will be high from suppliers/customers – some will take their business elsewhere
1–10	Poor	This is not a team – it is a collection of individuals with no cohesion. Radical actions are urgently needed to improve motivation. Your performance severely impairs other parts of the organisation. Nobody wants to do business with this team

You may like to identify two or three areas in which you and your team have given low scores. Drawing on your understanding of the impact of motivation on team effectiveness, consider remedies that could be applied before discussing these with your team and your boss.

If people are given the opportunity to contribute to team issues, they will be more committed to both their own and team objectives. However, remember that it takes time and effort to change from where the team is now to where you want it to be. Your role as the team leader is to provide people with the resources and opportunities to improve team effectiveness. Encouragement and feedback are essential if the process of improvement is to be successful and sustained.

Creating the conditions for results management

This section looks at some of the extrinsic factors that cause satisfaction or dissatisfaction at work – based on Herzberg's work. It looks at working conditions and examines working relationships at organisational and at team levels.

Physical conditions

Since the Industrial Revolution there has been a conflict between the needs of employers and the needs of workers. For example:

- ◆ Employers want to maximise productivity and keep costs to the minimum needed to grow their businesses. This might require staff to work in inappropriate, arduous or hazardous conditions for long hours and for low pay, with little or no benefits arising from their contributions to the wealth/growth generated by the organisation.

- ◆ Theme 2 gives you some indication of what employees want from their job. These may be at odds with what organisations are prepared to provide for their staff.

The Industrial Revolution introduced the widespread use of the factory system of operating – dividing up jobs into components with each person continuously reproducing part of the whole, rather than producing the whole article. It also took work away from worker's homes into dedicated factory units, as mechanisation took over from hand labour. Because of the insular attitude of employers towards working conditions and workers' rights, co-operatives, trade unions and workers' councils all developed to represent the collective views and needs of workers. These 'labour movements' in industrialised countries soon began to flex their muscles in a political manner, and workers' rights and conditions quickly became part of the wider political agenda. This political agenda has widened and deepened into what we know today as health, safety and welfare legislation.

Today, workers' rights are championed by a wide variety of organisations, such as:

- ◆ regional, national and local government organisations
- ◆ non-government organisations (NGOs) such as the World Bank, which is a major proponent of better working conditions in developing countries
- ◆ trade unions, workers' councils etc.

♦ campaign and pressure groups

♦ the press, TV and radio.

'Managers' should be added to this list of champions. Ensuring that working conditions for staff are safe and appropriate to the job is one of your prime responsibilities. This requires that a risk assessment be completed to ensure that all known risks are identified, measured and managed. Managers who fail to discharge their responsibilities for working conditions, including health and safety matters, may be liable to fines and imprisonment if found guilty of offences under national or international laws.

National and international standards apply to many industries, and organisations operating within some industries have to comply as a prerequisite for operating. For example, there are currently 556 different international standards regarding all aspects of production of the large number of base chemicals used as ingredients in many products which form part of our everyday lives, such as medicines, epoxies and plastics. These standards are co-ordinated by the International Organisation for Standardisation (ISO).

Many employers do 'walk the talk' when it comes to staff working conditions. Rules and regulations create a basic framework, but organisations are increasingly aware that if they look after their people, they will be more productive. Naturally, organisations also wish to benefit by promoting themselves as caring employers. One of the world's largest organisations, the Royal Dutch/Shell Group of Companies (Shell), makes its policies on health and safety in the western world clear, and also publishes annual statistics showing the commitment that lies behind its policies.

Royal Dutch/Shell Group of Companies, commitment to health, safety and the environment (HSE)
In the Group we are committed to:

♦ pursue the goals of no harm to people

♦ protect the environment

♦ use material and energy efficiently to provide our products and services

♦ develop energy resources, products and services consistent with these aims

♦ publicly report on our performance

♦ play a leading role in promoting best practices in our industries

♦ manage HSE matters as any other critical business activity

♦ promote a culture in which all Shell employees share this commitment.

The Royal Dutch/Shell Group of Companies HSE policy

Every Shell company:

- has a systematic approach to HSE management, designed to ensure compliance with the law and to achieve continuous performance improvement

- sets targets for improvements and measures, appraises and reports on performance

- requires contractors to manage HSE in line with this policy

- requires joint ventures under its operational control to apply this policy, and uses its influence to promote it in its other ventures

- includes HSE performance in the appraisal of staff and rewards accordingly.

Source: *Royal Dutch/Shell Group of Companies* (www)

Many aspects of Shell's commitment and policy impact directly on manager/team leader responsibilities.

Getting the basics right

Notwithstanding the example of Shell and other enlightened companies, there are still many organisations operating across the world today, and not all are in the emerging economies, that do not place staff health, safety and welfare high on their agenda. Such organisations are usually owned and operated by unscrupulous people whose sole aim is to squeeze as much out of their staff as possible in order to maximise profitability. Look at the following example:

An organisation exploited young graduate trainee staff by forcing them to work very long hours – until recently as many as 130 hours per week – and to be on continual shifts of up to 36 hours. The staff had to grab some sleep at work and be on call for all emergencies as well as routine work. The trainees revolted over their hours and conditions and asked their professional body to intervene. Previous requests had always met with the response, 'We had to do it so why shouldn't you'. However, the latest round of revolts caught the attention of the press and public, and the trainees were also supported by a few opposition politicians who made lots of noise. The outcome was that, over an agreed period of time, working hours would be reduced to no more than 80 per week, with both sides acknowledging the disruption and dangers that could arise if hours of work were reduced immediately. Note that there is also a skill shortage in this work area – but is this an excuse for treating people in such a poor fashion?

Where did this occur – in a low income, developing country with a track record of poor working conditions? No!

This situation occurred in the UK, where young doctors, recently qualified from medical schools, undertake mandatory periods of experience in hospitals across a wide range of medical disciplines. Their employer is the UK government, through its nationalised National Health Service. The doctors were either working or on call at hospitals for very long periods of time. What price their quality of life, their welfare (and the welfare of their patients) and the quality of decision making and medical expertise being practised daily/nightly throughout the UK? It was only because of publicity campaigns and working to rule (working the minimum number of hours stipulated in their contracts) that their employers and their professional body took note and agreed better terms and conditions.

Differences in working conditions

People work across the whole spectrum of industry and commerce and there are many who work in adverse, arduous, hazardous or unpleasant occupations so that others can enjoy a reasonable quality of life – for example in mining, fishing and construction. Many governments and the European Union have agreed that legislation and regulations on working conditions drawn up to protect the rights and interests of workers should be appropriate for that industry, and that organisations engaged in business within discrete industries have to comply with these laws and regulations. The argument that compliance causes an organisation to be at a disadvantage is spurious. The laws and regulations apply across industries, and so there should be no economic disadvantage to, say, incorporating new or upgraded safety systems at work.

Organisations operating internationally, for example, in capital construction and petrochemical industries, often adopt the regulations of their home country if the regulations in the overseas territory are less rigorous. This provides a consistent approach and enables mobile staff to operate with confidence wherever they are. It also acts as a spur to the local country to improve its approach to workers' conditions. Western organisations are mindful of the adverse publicity that could arise if they are seen to be exploiting labour in developing countries by providing working conditions that would not be acceptable in their home country. This is a different issue to that of exploiting low costs.

An example of the rise in consumer awareness about the need to improve worker conditions is given below:

Exporting Labor Standards

An editorial in the *Christian Science Monitor*, 6 March 2001, reports: The American firms that contract out manual labour to overseas factories are closely watched for how workers in those plants are treated. The companies know that US anti-sweatshop activists can quickly spark a consumer boycott with the first sign of worker abuse. So it's a sign of progress that a report on abuses in Indonesian factories used by shoe giant Nike is leading to remedy, not a big consumer revolt.

This extract was taken from the Nike website. The company has suffered adverse publicity and consumer reactions in the past regarding work conditions in some of its units in Asia. It takes these responsibilities very seriously, admits to its mistakes and publishes details about where it has gone wrong and the steps it has taken to remedy these situations.

Source: *Nike* (www)

The manager's role

Many people voluntarily work in adverse conditions, and when offered the opportunity to move to another job, often refuse because they enjoy their work and accept the conditions as part of the job. Your role in maintaining, improving and promoting good working conditions for your staff and all other staff who may work in or visit your area of responsibility is crucial.

Although representing the interests of staff regarding physical working conditions is a key part of your role, there is also much scope for you to play a proactive role in helping to create conducive working conditions through:

- ensuring fair play
- promoting open communications among your team up, down and across the organisation, so that dissatisfaction becomes apparent and can be acted on
- making work an enjoyable and fun place to be
- developing respect and trust
- developing staff relationships.

Ensuring fair play

Ensure fair play at all levels within your area of responsibility. At times you will be called upon to arbitrate in disputes between team members and between the team and others. In some circumstances you may have to represent the wishes or needs of the organisation, which may run counter to those of the team or individual members.

Such situations may cause a dilemma as you may have to ask yourself: 'Whose interests am I supposed to be representing here?' The answer is that you must always represent both sets of interests to ensure fair play.

Open communications

It should be obvious that maintaining open channels of communications will help managers to resolve, maintain or improve working conditions for staff. You must be tuned in to your environment and people. Your staff are your key resource, and you should pick up early warning signs of any problem or potential problems so you can deal with them before they blossom into major issues. A manager who is tuned in will also be able to act quickly to help improve matters before a formal request is made. Open communications also mean regular contact with other managers, especially those in the supply chain, and maintaining a current understanding of the broader organisational issues.

When issues that affect working conditions arise, involve the staff affected. People know their jobs, understand the situation and should be well placed to make pragmatic inputs. In collective bargaining situations, a representative from the trade union or workers' council may represent the interests of the affected group of workers.

Guidelines for dealing with dissatisfaction among your staff

◆ Hear what is being said (and what is not being said)

◆ Understand the issues and the background to the issues

◆ Determine whether the issues are causes or effects

◆ Decide whether you have the capability and authority to implement changes

◆ Seek help and guidance

◆ Keep staff informed of developments.

Work is enjoyable, fun

How much fun is your workplace? Here are some examples of people having fun at work, or in connection with work.

On 1 December each year, a senior manager in the London HQ of an international bank placed a simple game on the end of his desk. Everyone passing his desk, staff and visitors, was encouraged to play the game, which took no more than a few seconds. There was a charge for participation and the money went into a collecting box for a children's charity. Over the month nearly £1,000 was collected and the charity was grateful for the donation it received just before Christmas. Everyone had lots of fun, and the manager's involvement with people from all departments and of all grades improved dramatically.

Marathon running has become popular and large numbers of teams, sponsored by companies, participate in major city marathons around the world. In addition to the company sponsorship of entry fees, clothing, travel, time off work, etc., the participants collect large sums for charity.

In the financial district of London, many banks and finance houses have teams which meet and play each other regularly across a wide range of sports including football, cricket, hockey, squash, table tennis, five-a-side football and badminton. Matches are played in the evenings or at weekends and competition is usually fierce. Companies sponsor the competition trophies, and the sports equipment and clothing worn by their teams.

Your role in promoting enjoyment in the workplace can take many forms, depending upon the industry, the situation, the people and the culture of the team, department and organisation, etc. Some of the enjoyment experienced by people may be due to their social interactions and has little to do with work itself. But bear in mind that people who enjoy their work and the conditions that they work in tend to put more into their jobs and get more from their jobs than others.

Respect and trust

It is often said that respect has to be earned – it is not automatically given with the job title. But how do you build respect and trust in your team? People's respect for others is based on a complex set of criteria and values, some of which may be objective and some of which may be subjective. The knowledge or incidents from which respect is gained can be very different, even among a close-knit team.

This example shows six different situations which contributed towards the respect earned by a team leader from his team:

Situations that earned respect from team members for their team leader

Team member 1: 'The manager always listens to me. I feel I can talk to him. Last year he knew something was troubling me. I don't know how he found out, but I had some problems at home and just talking things through with him helped sort things out in my head.'

Team member 2: 'I like the way he deals with people. He is strict but fair and he also admits to being wrong if something is his fault. Another thing, he doesn't try to pretend that he knows it all. For example, John's job is highly specialised and the boss lets him get on with it.'

Team member 3: 'He is really tight with suppliers. He always backs us up when we reject components because of poor quality.'

Team member 4: 'He really knows his job – and mine. Whenever there is a problem he is always helpful – even if it is my fault. He says that every error is a learning event for everyone involved, but he doesn't expect too many of them and he certainly doesn't expect an error to be repeated.'

Team member 5: 'I had a problem with the human resources (HR) department, which was mucking around with my pay – it was always late into my bank account. He spoke to the HR manager and asked her to sort it out as it was affecting my work. I got a phone call and an apology the same day.'

Team member 6: 'My job changed last year and he spent loads of time with me, helping me to become familiar with the new equipment. I never felt under pressure, although I knew there was a backlog, which I cleared with a bit of overtime.'

The situations reported in the above example cover organisational issues, personal issues, inter-personal issues, dissatisfiers and development. The team leader builds respect by being interested in his people, supportive of them, fair and firm.

Working relationships

We can identify three levels at which initiatives are undertaken to promote productive and effective working relationships:

Level 1 Initiatives that meet or exceed government and industry standards

Level 2 Initiatives that the organisation puts in place, possibly influenced by industry, location or culture

Level 3 Initiatives between managers and staff

We will consider each of these levels.

Level 1

In the UK, within the Department of Trade and Industry, the Employment Relations Directorate is responsible for developing the framework for employers and employees to promote a skilled and flexible labour market founded on principles of partnership.

Ideas of partnership used to get short shrift from employees who felt that they had little or no influence over employers and over what could be improved within the workplace. It is becoming increasingly evident that senior managers now understand that many of the changes and innovations that they need to put in place to remain competitive and survive stem from staff involvement. It is this realisation that staff have much more to offer than simply producing work within their own, often narrow, job roles that has been one of the spurs for improving employment relationships at three distinct levels.

The framework for employment relations in the UK includes legislation covering the national minimum wage, pay and employment rights. The Employment Relations Act 1999 addresses issues such as workers' rights, ballots, recognition, workplace partnerships, tribunals and dispute resolution. It also covers work and parents, redundancy arrangements, employee consultation, and collective rights.

More information on all of these can be obtained from the UK Department of Trade and Industry website: www.dti.gov.uk/er

Level 2

Organisations may seek to enhance employee relations through a wide range of initiatives. Here are just a few:

◆ comprehensive rewards and benefits

◆ subsidised mortgage scheme

◆ discounted purchases of goods or services

◆ sharesave scheme in which shares can be bought at a discounted price

◆ subsidised restaurant

◆ sports and leisure facilities and/or sponsorship of sports teams/leisure activities

◆ protective clothing and uniforms

◆ private or subsidised medical/dental care

◆ flexible working arrangements and daycare for babies and young children

◆ staff development, including professional qualifications, college and university courses.

See the next section for more on rewards.

Level 3

We have already covered many of the initiatives to promote good working relationships between manager and staff. The secret here is that there is no secret; it is sound common sense and about valuing individuals and their contributions.

Put yourself in your team's shoes. What is it that you expect from your boss and what is it that you value from working relationships? This is often a good starting point, but remember it is only a starting point and some team members will have different needs.

Being a good manager is hard work. It means that you constantly have to juggle the needs of people, the organisation and the routine work that needs to be done, while achieving specific goals or objectives. However, nothing gets done except through people and this may be where you need to spend much of your time.

Motivators at work

Here are some ideas on motivators at work:

- Make work more active
- Build fun into work
- Add variety to work
- Facilitate employee involvement
- Let employees make more choices
- Increase responsibility (and authority)
- Facilitate teamwork
- Encourage learning and continuous improvement
- Let employees set their own goals
- Encourage self-measurement
- Establish an environment conducive to continuous employment
- Provide plenty of encouragement
- Create a climate of appreciation
- Help employees understand the significance of their work.

Source: *Spitzer* (1996)

Activity 8
Working conditions

Objective

This activity will help you to identify the scope of your responsibilities for working conditions.

Task

Do you know the full scope of your responsibilities for physical working conditions within your areas of responsibility? Without looking at any rule books, manuals, or talking with other people, etc., list your main responsibilities in the chart provided below.

Area	Responsibilities

Now check your rule books or manuals and add to or amend your list as appropriate. This is a good opportunity for you to refresh your understanding of your responsibilities – there is little point in refreshing your knowledge after an event! Bear in mind health and safety, fire and emergency responsibilities as well as the provision of training facilities and refresher courses.

Feedback

Where aspects of the working environment apply to or affect your team, then you have primary responsibility to ensure that they are implemented/maintained. For example, the building facilities manager may have overall responsibility for checking fire extinguishers, but if a fire occurred and the extinguishers didn't work, you might have trouble convincing anyone that it was not your responsibility – you just managed the team that occupied the space!

Linking rewards and results

While money is undoubtedly important, there is a lot more to rewarding staff than just money.

> In a survey conducted by Northwestern Mutual Life/Louis Harris, only a third of young workers who took part said salary was most important and many would not trade free time for higher pay and gruelling hours.

Source: *Cates and Rahimi* (2001)

> A survey commissioned by Reed Executive and the Chartered Institute of Personnel and Development shows that 91 per cent of UK workers would cut hours or pay to save their job and help their company survive any recession.

Source: *Cottell* (2001)

What rewards?

Rewards come in two forms:

- ◆ monetary rewards
- ◆ non-monetary rewards – both formal and informal.

Your organisation is likely to have a formal reward and compensation system – concerned primarily with monetary rewards – in which you may be involved, for example by making recommendations for compensation. However, your ability to influence the system may be limited. You are more likely to have influence over informal, non-monetary rewards. This power is not inconsequential. Spitzer (1996) suggests that 'sometimes a jelly doughnut or a handshake is as effective, if not more effective, than a monetary bonus'.

Monetary rewards

The list of monetary rewards typically offered by organisations can be split into direct monetary rewards and other monetary equivalent rewards which have cash values. Direct monetary rewards include:

- **Basic pay** – some organisations have a flat rate for jobs and job families, others agree rates of pay for the experience and skills which people bring to their jobs.
- **Incremental pay** – the basic rate of pay increases at agreed incremental points, for example, for each year of service in a particular grade/job. The problem with incremental pay is that people are rewarded for nothing other than time spent in the grade. A frequent criticism is that mediocrity is rewarded because average performers, who have greater seniority than gifted performers, get paid more.
- **Bonuses,** for example, at Christmas and the year end, in conjunction with a project completion, because targets have been met or exceeded.
- **Commission payments,** especially for sales staff. In some industries or companies it is common practice to incentivise sales staff by retaining them on a low basic salary and paying commissions on sales results.
- **Bonuses** for exemplary performance or for gaining a degree or professional qualification.
- **Profit sharing schemes,** for example, an annual bonus linked to company performance.

Some rewards are deferred, thereby encouraging talented employees to stay with the organsiation. For example:

- Pension schemes are offered by some organisations. These are either contributory schemes where people contribute towards their own pension fund or non-contributory schemes where the organisation makes all payments on behalf of staff.
- Share options, usually restricted to managers and key staff, are used not just as a reward, but also as a retention tool.
- Sharesave scheme, available to all staff in the companies which operate them.

Besides money, organisations may offer a vast range of monetary-equivalent rewards, such as insurance benefits, private health schemes, low-interest mortgages, cars or car allowances. In addition, they may operate incentive schemes with gift vouchers, travel or holidays as the reward.

Peter Drucker (1974) urges caution, highlighting that cash rewards can easily become rights.

Economic incentives are becoming rights rather than rewards. Merit raises are always introduced as rewards for exceptional performance. In no time at all, they become a right. To deny a merit raise or to grant only a small one becomes punishment. The increasing demand for material rewards is rapidly destroying their usefulness as incentives and managerial tools.

Source: *Drucker* 1974

Linking reward to performance

Several links can be made between reward and performance. Many organisations operate a policy of performance-related pay for all staff. How performance is measured and how reward is distributed varies widely, but there are some common considerations with which managers are closely involved.

The principle behind the example given in Figure 3.3 is that performance-related pay is often calculated on a number of variables, which include individual, team and overall performance.

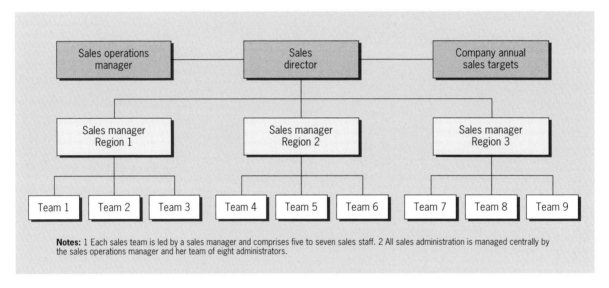

Figure 3.3 *Sales director's responsibilities*

Figure 3.3 is an example of a sales director's responsibilities. Starting with the sales director's objective to meet targeted sales for the next financial year, all of her managers' and staff's objectives should be written to ensure each contributes towards achievement of this objective. Contributions towards achievement of the overall target will be met in the following way:

◆ The sales director will agree with the operations manager what her targets should be to support sales

◆ The sales director will agree targets with his regional managers

◆ Regional managers will agree how their targets will be divided among their sales managers

◆ Sales managers will agree their team's targets, and how they should be divided among the team and themselves

◆ Individual sales staff will agree their targets.

Assuming everyone meets or exceeds their targets, then individual sales staff reward may be granted by calculating:

Individual performance

+ Team performance

+ Regional performance

+ Overall performance

= **Reward**

However, it might not be that simple. The reward gained may also be factored by the individual's overall contribution to the team/organisation, as determined by a reward appraisal. For example, one sales person may have significantly exceeded her targets simply by answering the phone when someone placed a large unsolicited order, but the sales manager may consider that her overall performance and contribution has been below par.

Rewards and control

In the example in Figure 3.3, also note that the sales managers have power to influence the rewards assigned to individuals. There is often a relationship between control and reward. Here is an example of this:

Organisations increasingly reward people with share options and share purchase schemes. However, these usually have a maturity date three to five years into the future, which means that the individual has to stick around for a defined period of time before they can cash their options and purchase their shares. The organisation's rationale is that it will be able to better manage (control) retention of staff, and one of the carrots (incentives) is that the value of the shares allocated at fixed prices should rise with the passage of time.

Individual versus team rewards

Many organisations reward individual performance even when they are actively promoting teamwork. This seems likely to hinder team motivation. Even if one individual has performed well, how might they have performed without the support and encouragement of the team, or if they had not been contributing towards the team goals? The following example illustrates problems with material rewards, such as cash, which have in some cases been found to have a demotivating effect and to impact negatively on team performance.

> Hughes Aircraft found certain aspects of the cash awards approach to be counterproductive. For example, cash awards reduced teamwork as employees concentrated primarily on individual cash gains. United Airlines dropped its long-time cash awards system because of litigation problems. Other companies noticed a negative boomerang effect whenever ideas were turned down. Many companies experienced ongoing problems with timely response and others noted disagreements on determining cash amounts, and conflicts regarding what constitutes a part of normal job performance. We have also found instances where 'pay' for certain types of intellectual performance tends to denigrate the performance and remove it from the intellectual achievement category, which elicits pride and satisfaction, and reduces it to a more mundane 'pay-for-performance' concept. We conclude that cash awards seem to have an overall demotivating effect.

Managers have to make their own judgements, based on objective measurement and observation, on how much an individual has contributed to the team goals and the manner in which this contribution has been made. For example, an individual may contribute willingly or grudgingly. A willing contributor will portray a very different demeanour from a grudging contributor, and it is the effect this demeanour has on the remainder of the team that the manager will take into consideration when determining the individual's overall performance.

Team rewards are commonplace in many industries and should promote all that is good and expected from effective teamworking. Incentives in many different forms, such as holidays, flights, vouchers with cash values, etc., are given.

> An excellent example is from Richer Sounds in the UK. This is an independent audio-visual company, mainly selling low-priced hi-fi equipment. Its retail outlets cover most of the UK and, among other things, the staff at the best performing store are given free use of the owner's Rolls Royce car for a week.

Non-monetary rewards

Non-monetary rewards include job titles, office furniture or workspace size, access to preferential car parking or corporate entertainment. The extent to which these rewards are coveted may well depend on the organisation's culture.

In one organisation, for example, the workers on the ground floor were provided with drinking water in plastic cups from a large cooled water dispenser. As you climbed to higher floors of the office building and reached the heights of director level, the cups became crystal glasses and the water was in small glass bottles. However, the cafeteria provided good-quality food and was used by staff of all levels in the organisation.

Organisations may also operate award schemes, for example an employee of the month award. Certificates, plaques or such like may become highly sought after and provide incentives.

Of course, the intrinsic qualities of the job can be highly rewarding, as we saw in the section **Motivation in practice.**

Informal rewards

As a manager you have scope to provide informal rewards as a way of motivating people. Informal rewards should be:

◆ directly to reinforce the desired behaviour – it needs to be clear that the reward is given in response to the desired behaviour

◆ immediate in their use – the reward needs to be given as soon as possible after the desired behaviour occurs

◆ delivered personally

◆ valued by the individual.

Knowing what individuals value is all a matter of getting to know your people and how they react in certain situations. It's also about finding out about their expectations of you as their manager.

Here are some ideas.

Praise people, for example, say 'well done', 'great job', 'thanks very much for that' (whatever 'that' may be). Such informal recognition will be reinforced if it is mentioned publicly at team briefing sessions or in the individual's workplace within the hearing of their co-workers.

Give people time off, allowing them to flex their hours and acknowledging that when they are at work they produce high value. However, do not favour some individuals over others as this could be detrimental to good relationships with other employees.

Give individuals and teams more involvement in problem solving and decision making.

Get your senior manager or a director to thank people personally or to write to them to thank them for outstanding work – make sure that others know. Such actions should be over and above anything that you do with the individuals. A written note is very useful as a motivator because a team will display it in a prominent position.

Celebrate success with the team – buy a round of coffee or supply a tray of doughnuts, or take them to the pub after work. The gesture doesn't have to be grand – just sincere.

The effectiveness of such rewards can be traced to the principles of positive reinforcement. This is effective because:

♦ The workers' response to the manager's positive reinforcement produces a consequence from the workers, which results in an increase in the frequency of their response (more good work, etc.).

♦ Any adverse emotional responses associated with punishment and extinction are apt to be reduced and, in fact, favourable emotions may be elicited. In other words, if a manager practises positive reinforcement, any negative views they express or disciplinary action they then take will be accepted much more positively by the recipients.

These informal rewards operate under the expectancy theory of motivation, which suggests that desired behaviour in a work setting is increased if a person perceives a positive relationship between effort and performance. The behaviour is further increased if there is a positive relationship between good performance and rewards, particularly if the rewards are valued.

Rewards linked to results

How motivational is your organisation's reward strategy? Is it geared to getting the results you need? Consider the following questions:

♦ Do employees feel that meritorious performance is consistently rewarded?

♦ Does your organisation's reward system send clear and unambiguous messages to employees about what is really important?

♦ Is 'getting the right results' rewarded much more frequently than 'getting to work'?

♦ Do employees get excited about the rewards your organisation offers?

♦ Do your employees feel adequately recognised for their efforts?

♦ Does your organisation reward employees' contributions promptly and creatively?

♦ Do employees have input into the rewards they receive?

♦ Do employees perceive the reward system in your organisation as being fair and objective?

Source: *Spitzer* (1996)

Spitzer (1996) suggests that rewards should:

♦ foster the desired outcomes of the organisation

♦ make people feel good about their current and past accomplishments

♦ energise them to achieve even more

♦ work synergistically with intrinsic motivation

♦ do these things cost-effectively.

Spitzer is by no means a lone voice calling for organisations and managers to link reward systems to the results that they value.

However, research by the Chartered Institute for Personnel and Development (CIPD) found that traditional and safe compensation systems, for example those that reward level and length of time in service rather than primarily performance and results, continue to predominate (CIPD, 2001). Spitzer's argument is that organisations are missing the opportunity to make the reward system motivational.

The activities that follow examine the range of rewards available to you and your team and rewards to enhance teamworking.

Activity 9
Rewards

Objectives

This activity will help you to:

◆ understand and confirm the range of rewards offered by your organisation

◆ confirm the range of informal rewards available to you and used by you to reward your team and individuals.

Task

Consider the following table of rewards that are commonly offered by organisations. How does your organisation compare and how many of these rewards offered by your organisation are available to you? If the reward is available, answer 'Yes'. If it is available, but not to you, answer 'X'. If it is not available in your organisation, answer 'No'.

Rewards commonly offered by organisations	Available in your organisation		
Monetary rewards	*Yes*	*X*	*No*
Basic pay	☐	☐	☐
Incremental pay	☐	☐	☐
Annual performance bonuses	☐	☐	☐
Commission payments	☐	☐	☐
Bonuses for exemplary performance or for gaining a degree or professional qualification	☐	☐	☐
Contributory pension scheme	☐	☐	☐
Non-contributory pension scheme (organisation pays your contributions)	☐	☐	☐
Share options	☐	☐	☐
Sharesave/purchase scheme	☐	☐	☐
Insurance benefits, e.g. accident or death payments	☐	☐	☐
Private health schemes for staff and family members	☐	☐	☐
Cars or car allowances for non-essential users	☐	☐	☐
Telephones, mobile phones and cost of calls	☐	☐	☐
Discounts on company products/services	☐	☐	☐
Low-interest mortgages/loans	☐	☐	☐
Gift vouchers, travel, holidays (part of incentive schemes)	☐	☐	☐

Rewards commonly offered by organisations	Available in your organisation		
Non-monetary rewards	*Yes*	*X*	*No*
Available in your organisation	☐	☐	☐
Job and job title	☐	☐	☐
Status within and external to the organisation	☐	☐	☐
Favourable location, size of office/workspace, office furniture	☐	☐	☐
Benefits which accompany grades, e.g. car parking, access to corporate entertainment (supposedly for customers)	☐	☐	☐
Class of travel by rail (standard or first), by air (economy, business or first)	☐	☐	☐
Recognition by superiors and peers	☐	☐	☐
Promotion/advancement	☐	☐	☐
Job widening	☐	☐	☐
Award of certificates, plaques (e.g. employee of the month)	☐	☐	☐
Increase in level of empowerment, authority	☐	☐	☐
Getting onto the succession planning chart – indicates potential	☐	☐	☐
Being considered as a 'high potential' employee, which may provide a fast track to certain management positions	☐	☐	☐
Selection for projects, certain key positions	☐	☐	☐
Selection for prestigious courses/programmes	☐	☐	☐
Sense of ownership in the role	☐	☐	☐
Sense of pride – level of satisfaction	☐	☐	☐

Feedback

How did your organisation score? The list is taken from a range of options offered by several organisations, therefore your organisation may not offer them all. Note that the last two options in the list are about how you feel, and so could be described as rewards/outcomes of the previous options.

If you consider that your organisation is below par on the range of rewards available, you may wish to discuss this with your boss. Whether you are eligible for some of these rewards is another matter. Some will be grade and performance dependent and it is a fact that the better you are at your job and the further you climb up the ladder, the greater the range of rewards you will be eligible for which are linked to the value the organisation places on you. But what about your staff – are you sure that you are providing them with the right level and nature of rewards to match their individual and team contributions?

Enlightened employers are taking great care to ensure that their employees' reward packages are as effective as possible. Organisations need to retain good staff and an effective rewards system is a key element in achieving this.

Activity 10
Rewarding the team

Objective

This activity will help you to review the type of rewards you can provide to enhance teamworking.

Task

The chart lists rewards and reinforcements you may be able to provide for your team to help develop their motivation and improve their efforts. Look at each one and decide whether:

◆ I do provide this

◆ I should provide this more frequently

◆ I cannot provide this, but I would like to be able to.

Reward	Do provide	Should provide more	Like to provide
Praise for a job well done	☐	☐	☐
Encouragement and support	☐	☐	☐
Freedom in how to undertake key tasks	☐	☐	☐
Delegation of stretching work	☐	☐	☐
Training and development opportunities	☐	☐	☐
Status symbols	☐	☐	☐
Time off/early finishes	☐	☐	☐
The chance to be more creative	☐	☐	☐
Showing gratitude/saying 'thank you'	☐	☐	☐
More challenging tasks	☐	☐	☐
Acclaim, e.g. employee of the month	☐	☐	☐
Authority over people or projects	☐	☐	☐
A good performance review	☐	☐	☐
Gifts, prizes, days out, social events	☐	☐	☐
A share in decision making	☐	☐	☐
Recommendations at a higher level	☐	☐	☐
The chance to work in other teams	☐	☐	☐
Constructive feedback	☐	☐	☐
Having their ideas acted on	☐	☐	☐
Favourite work	☐	☐	☐
Clearer goals and targets	☐	☐	☐
Having more control of a situation	☐	☐	☐
Being assigned a mentor	☐	☐	☐

Feedback

Clearly the more ticks you have in the first column the better. You may find that there are too many ticks in the middle column. In other words, there are rewards that are within your power to provide, but which you don't give often enough. This may be because of time, the location of the team or because you feel uncomfortable giving these rewards. Consider ways that you could improve your performance in these areas.

The final column is a bit more of a challenge. It is likely that there are some things you cannot provide. If you can't influence these things, concentrate on the others. It may be that a discussion with your own manager could lead to change. They may not realise that it would help your team performance if you could reward individuals in these ways.

You may have noticed that most of the rewards are to do with rewarding individual rather than team performance. This is because people see rewards in very different ways. For example, someone who is rewarded by having their achievements recognised by you may hate the idea of standing up in public to receive an employee of the month award. The challenge for you is to find out what motivates individuals on your team and to select an appropriate reward for them.

◆ Recap

Use techniques to help you identify and understand the causes of motivation and demotivation

- ◆ A manager has a range of techniques and rewards available to support motivation in the team. These include: extrinsic factors such as salary, security, status, working conditions, opportunities for development; intrinsic factors such as job satisfaction, autonomy, clarity of goals, the identity of the job.

- ◆ There are also factors associated with job design and teamworking.

Benchmark your team's performance against some characteristics of high-performing teams

- ◆ You need to have a vision of where you want your team to be and understands the behaviours and attitudes that will make it a high-performing team.

- The motivational and performance characteristics that may make a difference include respect, trust, commitment, enjoyment of work and leadership.

Identify the scope of your responsibilities for working conditions

- Your role in identifying satisfiers and dissatisfiers at work is fundamental to your being able to make a difference to working conditions.

- The working conditions on which you can have an impact may vary considerably, but could include ensuring fair play, listening, open communications, making work fun and enjoyable, and ensuring health and safety.

Understand the range of formal and informal rewards available to you for use with your team

- Rewards come in two forms: monetary and non-monetary. Money is by no means the only effective motivator.

- As a manager you need to be aware of your capacity to offer rewards such as commissions and bonuses, team and individual rewards, valuing individuals, listening, providing feedback, praise, new job titles, office space, job enlargement, certificates, empowerment, etc.

 **More @**

Mullins, L. J. (1999) 5th edition, *Management and Organisational Behaviour*, FT Pitman Publishing
Taking a managerial approach and demonstrating the application of behavioural science within the workplace, this text emphasises the role of management as a core integrating activity. This is a long-established text that is accessible in style and clear in presentation, by making unfamiliar theory relevant, easily understood and logically applied to the world of work.

Stredwick, J. (2000) *An Introduction to Human Resource Management*, Elsevier Butterworth-Heinemann
This is a comprehensive and wide-ranging text which examines all the major aspects of human resource management in a down-to-earth and practical way. Chapter 8 looks at performance management, raising and measuring performance and operational issues around performance management. Chapter 9 examines rewards for employees, including pay structures and benefits. Chapter 11 looks at health, safety and welfare.

Thomson, R. (2002) 3rd edition, *Managing People*, Elsevier Butterworth-Heinemann
Managing People addresses the perspective of the individual manager whose role includes the management of people as well as issues concerning the organisation as a whole. See particularly Chapter 5 'Motivation, job satisfaction and job design' and Chapter 8 'Managing performance'.

Tyson, S. and York, A. (2000) 4th edition, *Essentials of HRM*, Elsevier Butterworth-Heinemann
Essentials of HRM combines an overview of organisational behaviour with a detailed explanation of human resource management policies and techniques. It also acts as an introduction to the study of industrial relations. There are a number of sections relevant to this theme including in Part 4: 'Assessing performance and managing careers' Chapter 11; 'Job evaluation' Chapter 13; 'Pay and benefits' Chapter 14; 'Conditions of service' Chapter 15.

www.cipd.co.uk and www.cbi.org.uk
For information about reward strategies you could visit the Chartered Institute for Personnel and Development's website – www.cipd.co.uk. For information on best practice try the Confederation of British Industry's website – www.cbi.org.uk

Full references are provided at the end of the book.

4 Grievance and disciplinary procedures

Do you know how the grievance process works in your organisation? Do you know how it is linked to individual motivation and performance? Can you differentiate between when a grievance is best managed at an informal level and when to apply the formal organisational procedure? In this theme we address what grievances are, grievance handling, how a generic grievance process operates and the impact of grievances on individuals and teams.

Disciplinary procedures are a fact of life and it is important to apply them promptly, sensitively and appropriately. This theme looks at informal and formal disciplinary actions and at how to make discipline a positive tool in your efforts to achieve results. Here we define dissatisfaction, complaint and grievance and differentiate between them to ensure that your response to, and handling of, each situation encountered is effective.

> **A happy worker is usually a productive worker.**

This theme looks at ways to use systems and processes appropriately and still achieve results. You will:

- ◆ Explore how the grievance process operates in your organisation to help you deal with conflict or poor quality of work

- ◆ Explore the way in which the disciplinary process operates in your organisation and find ways to deal with disciplinary matters promptly and effectively

- ◆ Identify situations in which an informal approach to discipline is effective and when to use the formal procedures

- ◆ Find out how to conduct a formal disciplinary interview.

The grievance process and links to results management

What does grievance mean? Pose this question to 10 people and you will probably get 10 different answers. However, a common differentiation between dissatisfaction, complaint and grievance, published by Pigors and Myers (1977), is shown in Table 4.1.

Dissatisfaction
Anything that disturbs an employee whether or not the unrest is expressed in words

Complaint
A spoken or written dissatisfaction brought to the attention of the team leader, supervisor, manager, or worker/union representative

Grievance
A complaint that has been formally presented to a management representative or to a union official

Table 4.1 *Understanding grievance*   Source: *Pigors and Myers* (1977)

Table 4.1 provides a useful framework for defining grievance. It is a serious or formal complaint and is not to be confused with grumbling or routine complaints.

Dissatisfaction and complaints

Dissatisfaction needs to be brought to your attention to give you the opportunity to understand and deal with the causes and to discuss the issues with staff. Furthermore, unresolved dissatisfaction may ultimately lead to complaints and grievances, including industrial unrest. Mullins (1999) suggests that much dissatisfaction evaporates overnight or after a short period of time. Life goes on and people do feel differently about matters after a period away from the source of dissatisfaction, or after a period of reflection.

In some organisations, complaints from staff are commonplace and are often associated with working conditions or extrinsic factors which are annoying them or preventing them from working effectively. Examples include machine or computer breakdowns, late supply of materials, inequitable workloads, impossible deadlines and non-functioning air conditioning. In many circumstances, individuals try to rectify the situation themselves, only complaining to their boss when nothing happens so that their boss uses his or her authority to get things moving.

Dealing with complaints and dissatisfaction
As a manager you should usually seek to deal with routine complaints or expressions of dissatisfaction unless, of course, the complaint is against you. Make sure you are clear about what response the complainants expect from you, and keep staff informed about what you can and can't do and the action you are taking to resolve the issue. Your involvement should enable a speedy resolution to the problem and should reaffirm your authority and competence.

It may be worth seeking advice from your line manager or a trusted colleague on how to deal effectively with a complaint.

> Make a note of your discussions and outcomes, and forward a copy to the HR department to be placed on the individual's personal file.

Fortunately, grievances occur rarely in most organisations and when they do they are usually given proper consideration. Some common issues which might arise in a grievance include the following:

- terms and conditions of employment
- health and safety issues
- relationships at work (often with the boss)
- new or changed working practices
- organisational change
- equal opportunities
- discrimination or harassment based on sex, race or disability.

Because of the seriousness and the implications of grievances, some organisations' policies stipulate that grievances be passed to the human resources department to co-ordinate the organisation's actions and responses.

Whatever the merits of the individual's grievance and the rights of individuals to air grievances, the harsh reality is that they may be stigmatised because of it. It might be that their current work situation becomes untenable, especially if they have complained about a co-worker or you. People who submit grievances often have to deal with the wider consequences as well as the outcomes of the grievance itself.

Grievance procedures

In any organisation, staff may have problems or concerns about their work, relationships at work or the working environment that they wish to raise and have addressed. A grievance procedure provides the mechanism for these to be dealt with fairly and speedily, before they develop into major problems and potentially into collective disputes.

In the UK, organisations are not required to have a grievance procedure, but it is good employment relations practice to provide staff with a reasonable and prompt opportunity to air their grievance, and have it fully considered.

However, employers are required by law to specify in their written statement of terms and conditions of employment a person or position holder to whom members of staff can make representation if they have a grievance. The employer is also required by law to allow the person submitting a grievance to be accompanied at certain grievance hearings – which we will discuss below.

Essential features of grievance processes

The grievance processes should be simple and straightforward. Grievance procedures should:

- be written down and communicated to all staff
- outline the steps that will be taken
- be undertaken in a prompt manner – the written proceedure should state the need for reacting to, and dealing with, the grievance promptly
- provide for confidentiality
- outline the procedure for the handling of grievance proceedings
- be fair and be seen to be fair
- confirm the individual's rights to hearings and rights of appeal against decisions taken.

The procedures in operation

The formal procedures differ between organisations, but they typically involve the following:

Stage 1. Staff convey their grievance to their manager, preferably in writing but it may be oral. If the grievance is reported orally, make a note of the details. Where the grievance is against the manager, it should be raised with the manager's own line manager. If the organisation contests the grievance, the member of staff should be invited to attend a hearing. In the UK, the Employment Relations Act 1999 stipulates that the individual has a right to be accompanied by a representative of their choice to grievance hearings that concern the performance of a duty by an employer in relation to the member of staff. For example, contract commitments that are being contested, such as the individual's right to a pay rise which is stipulated in a contract but which hasn't been awarded.

You should respond to the grievance within a specified time (for example, five days). If this is not possible, for example, because investigations into the grievance are continuing, the individual should be informed and told when a response may be expected.

Stage 2. If the matter is not resolved at Stage 1, the member of staff should be allowed to raise the matter in writing with a more senior manager. The choice of senior manager will depend on the organisation, but would typically be a divisional director or the head of a business unit. This manager should agree to hear the matter within a specified time (for example, five days). Following the hearing, the manager should respond in writing within a specified time (5–10 days). Again, if this is not possible, the member of staff should be told the reasons why and informed of when a response should be expected.

Final stage. If the matter remains unresolved, the individual has a final right to a hearing with another senior manager. This may not be possible in small organisations where there are only two or three layers of management. The process is the same as before. When grievances reach this stage, some organisations ask for external assistance in resolving them, perhaps if relations have broken down or to ensure impartiality.

Harassment and discrimination

Some organisations have implemented special procedures to deal with grievances involving infringement of equal opportunities and which may involve harassment or discrimination. In the UK and many other countries, there are laws governing these issues and employers must act within the law at all times, especially to maintain and protect workers' rights. Some organisations have collected all aspects of equal opportunities under a unified policy which embraces:

- equal pay
- sex discrimination
- racial discrimination
- discrimination against disabled persons
- harassment at work
- ageism (often to protect older people).

People have a right to protection from unwelcome attention or words that may constitute harassment. In general terms, under English law, harassment is unwanted conduct affecting the dignity of men and women in the workplace. It may be related to age, sex, religion, disability, nationality or any personal characteristic of the individual. It may be persistent or isolated. The key is that the actions or comments are viewed as demeaning and unacceptable to the recipient.

Harassment in the workplace is probably one of the most publicised areas of harassment law. The media often carry stories of cases heard in employment tribunals, usually involving racial or sexual harassment. Until 1997, there was no specific legislation in the UK for dealing with harassment, so cases were tried under the respective sex and racial discrimination laws. The Protection from Harassment Act 1977 now deals with these and wider issues of harassment.

Bullying

Regrettably, bullying does occur in the workplace. It can take several different forms and may include harassment or discriminatory behaviour. Examples include:

- spreading malicious rumours or insulting someone (particularly on gender/race/disability grounds)
- copying memos that are critical of someone to others who do not need to know
- ridiculing or demeaning someone – picking on them or setting them up to fail
- exclusion or victimisation
- unfair treatment
- overbearing supervision or other misuse of power or position
- unwelcome sexual advances – touching, standing too close, displaying offensive materials
- making threats or comments about job security without foundation
- deliberately undermining a competent worker by overloading and constant criticism
- preventing individuals from progressing by intentionally blocking promotion or training opportunities.

As with harassment, individuals may react differently to comments or actions, so that what might constitute firm management in the mind of one recipient may be construed as bullying by another.

Neither bullying nor harassment need be face to face with the individual. Both can occur through a variety of communications mediums, including comments made about people in their absence.

The importance of taking action

Bullying and harassment are not only unacceptable on moral grounds but may, if unchecked or handled badly, create serious problems for your organisation, including:

- poor morale and poor employee relations
- loss of respect for managers and supervisors
- poor performance and lost productivity

> ◆ damage to the organisation's reputation
>
> ◆ tribunal and other court cases and payment of unlimited compensation.

It is in every employer's interests to promote a safe, healthy and fair environment in which people can work and this means attending to harassment and bullying.

Constructive dismissal/employment tribunals

If an individual feels that their grievance is so serious that they have no other option than to leave the organisation, they may sue for damages because of constructive dismissal. This and other cases of grievance are often dealt with by employment tribunals that are open to the public and the media. Managers' testimony, involvement, comments and actions often form a core element of the cases. This level of investigation and arbitration can be damaging to the staff and managers involved and can attract adverse publicity for the organisation. These tribunals often portray the fallibility of managers who were unwilling or unable to discharge their responsibilities correctly.

Managers and grievances

Many grievances aired by staff, and some managers, arise because of situations beyond the capability or authority of the manager involved, such as a dispute over pay or other terms and conditions. We mentioned earlier the stigma attached to people who raise grievances, and the harsh reality of the difficulties sometimes encountered while trying to continue to work after a grievance has been raised and dealt with. Sometimes managers turn a blind eye or acquiesce in the unacceptable behaviour of their staff in the mistaken belief that it will go away if ignored. Stigma sometimes also attaches to the manager involved. It may be that, in certain circumstances, perceptions or views are held regarding the manager's handling of the situation. Such perceptions or views usually relate to the early warning signs that senior managers feel should have been addressed to remedy the situation when dissatisfaction or complaints were first raised. You could use the following checklist of action to help you address staff dissatisfaction, complaints or grievances right from the start.

Grievance-handling checklist for managers

1 Be aware of signs of dissatisfaction, for example:

- ◆ grumbling or dissent – voiced openly or behind people's backs

- ◆ lack of motivation, poor timekeeping, low-quality work.

2 Act promptly and fairly in response to any complaint made to you.

3 Keep HR informed from the early stages.

4 Consider holding discussions with the individuals involved and those on the periphery.

5 Seek advice from other managers, for example your boss or a specialist, throughout the process, and act on advice where appropriate.

6 Find out the facts about the complaint/grievance – by yourself or by involving other people.

7 Keep the individual regularly informed of the actions you are taking to determine the facts or remedy the situation – don't sit on a problem, take prompt action.

8 Make written notes about incidents and the timing of events, your discussions with the people involved, the established facts and your actions.

9 Pass a copy of your notes to the HR department to be placed on record.

10 Make sure any decisions you make are fair and correct – draw on advice.

11 If the situation involves a grievance procedure:

- ◆ act speedily

- ◆ ensure the rights of the individual are upheld, for example, notify them of their rights, including the right to be accompanied at a hearing (if appropriate)

- ◆ keep them informed of progress.

If you are asked to appear before a senior manager or tribunal to account for your actions, you will want to be completely satisfied that at all times and in all circumstances you acted properly and fairly.

Nobody enjoys dealing with dissatisfaction, complaints and, especially, grievances. However, some level of dissatisfaction with the status quo might be interpreted as an opportunity for the organisation to rectify a situation, or to change or improve processes that improve working conditions for staff. A happy worker is usually a productive worker.

Activity 11
Grievance handling

Objectives

This activity will help you to:

◆ develop your understanding of a situation that led to a grievance

◆ determine your own responses to a grievance situation – what you need to know and what options are open to you.

Case study

Read the case study before you complete the task.

Bob is a maintenance technician in a large engineering company that works 24/7 for 50 weeks of the year. Maintenance is essential to the smooth running of engineering operations. The company invests heavily in planned maintenance and Bob is always busy checking and replacing equipment as well as fixing breakdowns. During the shutdown period, the maintenance staff, supplemented by staff from other plants, undertake wholescale maintenance of the plant. Bob and some other members of his team also spend four weeks of the year undertaking shutdown maintenance in other plants. These are extremely busy periods, planned to a fine degree and the maintenance staff work long hours, for which they are well rewarded. The dates are known well in advance and there is a leave block for the maintenance team over these periods.

When Bob was asked by his team leader which off-site secondment he wished to do, Bob responded that because of his daughter's ongoing medical condition, he needed to stay close to home. He then explained that her doctor was waiting for her condition to stabilise because she needed to undergo a major operation. His team leader said that he understood fully and would not write Bob into the secondment schedule, and that if there was anything else he could do, Bob should talk with him.

Bob was much heartened by his team leader's responses and discussed it with the rest of his team at the next break. His teammates were all very sympathetic to Bob, most of them also had young children and they gave Bob and his wife their full support. As far as the team was concerned it was a 'no brainer' – Bob had to be near to his daughter and they would cover the secondments, knowing that Bob would do the same for any of them. A few weeks later, Bob's team leader approached Bob and said that he needed him to go on the next secondment for a few days. Bob said that it was impossible, his daughter was still in a bad way and he was needed at home, and that if necessary he would obtain a letter from her doctor. His team leader said that Bob had to go, otherwise he would put the whole shutdown of the other plant in jeopardy. Bob said the team leader was being ridiculous and needed to find another option as he wasn't going. The next day, the team leader took Bob off his routine maintenance work and told him to clean up the maintenance department, complaining that it was a right mess. Bob did the work uncomplainingly and went back to his normal duties after a few hours.

The following week, the team leader told Bob that he was still rostered for the secondment and that he needed to make other arrangements for his family – as far as the team leader was concerned the job came first. Bob reiterated that he would not go, could not go and that he would produce a doctor's letter as evidence. The team leader's response was to laugh and say that he knew all about people like Bob obtaining doctor's letters when it suited them. This made Bob very angry and he decided to walk away from the team leader, who kept shouting after him. After a couple of hours, one of Bob's co-workers said that he was to report immediately to the maintenance manager's office. Bob went to the office and found the manager and his team leader there. He was told by the maintenance manager that undertaking the secondments was an essential element of working as a maintenance technician and that Bob would have to undertake his fair share. Bob tried to respond, but he was told that he could take it or leave it, but that he would have to suffer the severe consequences if he didn't go on secondment. The manager then said that Bob should think about it, but that he was sure Bob would see what needed to be done.

Bob couldn't believe what he had heard. All sorts of things were going through his head and he couldn't think clearly – what he thought had just been said was that his job was on the line. He asked if this was the case and the manager replied, 'Yes'. Bob then turned to his team leader and asked him about their conversation earlier in the year in which the team leader had offered all support. The team leader merely replied that the job had to come first. The manager concluded the meeting by telling Bob that he had 24 hours in which to decide where his future lay.

Bob thought about approaching his union representative, but after successive rounds of redundancies, the union representative and the rest of the members were more concerned about hanging on to their jobs than making waves. What had occurred over the past few years, both through changed legislation and the apathy of the workers, was that the union position had become very weak and only really operated effectively in collective bargaining at the annual pay round.

Bob went back to the maintenance team's rest room and bumped into his friend, Phil, who asked what was going on as he had heard that Bob had been called to the manager's office. Bob told him and Phil became very angry. He immediately made a phone call and outlined the circumstances to the other person. Phil then asked Bob if he would be available to go to a meeting after work and Bob said yes, provided he phoned his wife. Phil was taking Bob to meet his brother-in-law who was senior manager of employee relations at a nearby company.

Task

Before answering the questions, you should first find out how the grievance process works within your own organisation. There should be a clearly defined policy and process guidance for all staff to follow, together with guidance notes for team leaders and managers on how to deal with grievances.

Who would be the subject of Bob's grievance?

To whom should Bob submit his grievance?

If you were Bob – what remedies would you request in your grievance submission?

Feedback

Here are some ideas.

Bob should submit a formal grievance against his team leader. He may also decide to submit a grievance against the maintenance manager. Although the maintenance manager has acted badly, we don't know what was discussed between him and the team leader. The maintenance manager may not know all of the facts or he may have been misled by the team leader. It is possible that a grievance against him would not be upheld.

Three options open to Bob in submitting his grievance are as follows:

◆ He could submit it to the maintenance manager (if he does not submit a grievance against him), or the maintenance manager's boss.

◆ He could submit it to an HR manager who should provide impartial advice and ensure the matter is dealt with speedily and effectively.

◆ He could involve his union representative who would probably advise him to submit it direct to the head of HR. If the local representative has no experience of advising people in grievance situations, the area or national organisation will probably have specialist advisors who would help Bob present his case. The union would probably be keen to assist as its involvement could help strengthen its position within the company.

Bob's grievance should ask for:

◆ removal from the secondment roster as per his original request that was agreed by the team leader, and which is now confirmed by a doctor's letter

- ◆ a verbal apology from the team leader

- ◆ a verbal apology from the maintenance manager (if a grievance is submitted against him)

- ◆ a written assurance from an appropriate senior manager (divisional director) that this incident will not affect his position or future within the company.

In the real world, if a grievance is upheld against a manager who has acted badly towards a member of staff, the organisation will keep a close watch on the future conduct of that manager, and in some cases formal disciplinary action may be appropriate. Many grievance situations start as dissatisfaction or complaints, but escalate because they have not been addressed properly.

If a member of your staff is dissatisfied and then complains about an individual or situation, you should do everything possible to prevent it escalating into a grievance – this will save you time and effort while maintaining a good relationship.

Activity 12
Dissatisfaction, complaint or grievance?

Objective

This activity will help you to distinguish between dissatisfaction, complaints and grievances within the workplace.

Task

Listed in the chart are some occurrences that we would like you to consider and then rate as:

Dissatisfaction   D

Complaint   C

Grievance   G

Occurrence	D	C	G
1 There is always a queue of cars waiting to get into and out of the company car park. It's really frustrating and adds another 30 minutes to the working day	☐	☐	☐
2 On several occasions recently there has been no toilet paper in the toilets and people have had to find other toilets to use	☐	☐	☐
3 A team member has a real problem with bad body odour	☐	☐	☐
4 Your promotion promised by the manager has not materialised	☐	☐	☐
5 The boss has cancelled your planned absence for a training course as the department is really busy	☐	☐	☐

Occurrence		D	C	G
6	There never seem to be enough clean cups in the office	☐	☐	☐
7	You discover that another manager has been bad-mouthing you behind your back and you believe this has affected a promotion which was promised, but hasn't materialised	☐	☐	☐
8	Your manager never seems to be around to talk to you and he has cancelled three agreed meetings. You made a mistake yesterday because you are using new equipment for which you haven't been trained and the manager's response was just to shout at you in front of the whole team	☐	☐	☐
9	You discover that everyone else on your team has been given higher bonuses than you, but your overall performance appraisal is better than some of theirs. Your manager's response is that it is a confidential process and that bonuses are discretionary – if you are not happy, then tough	☐	☐	☐
10	Since a new catering manager took over, the quality of the food in the staff restaurant has gone down to the point that people are not going there any more. The management response is that if people don't use the restaurant, the quality can't rise because the income is insufficient	☐	☐	☐
11	The cabling underneath desks is very untidy and on three occasions yesterday PCs were accidentally disconnected from the server as people trod on cables	☐	☐	☐
12	You have been asked to do an extra security check of the building at the end of the day because of a colleague's unexplained absence – which means that you leave work 20 minutes later than normal	☐	☐	☐
13	Your manager is always on at you: he shouts, swears and makes scenes. You feel threatened by his behaviour, but others in your team just tell him to get lost. It's been happening for a while and despite another manager telling him to back off, he still persists in hounding you	☐	☐	☐
14	The coffee machine has broken down and a replacement part is not available until the day after tomorrow. The nearest machine is on the next floor	☐	☐	☐

Feedback

Your responses may differ from ours, depending on a combination of:

♦ your own views/needs and management style

♦ the culture of your organisation

♦ the situation

♦ the people involved.

No.	Response	No.	Response	No.	Response
1	D	6	D	11	C
2	C	7	G	12	D
3	C	8	C	13	G
4	D	9	G	14	D
5	D	10	C		

You will find it worthwhile to discuss with your colleagues what they consider to be dissatisfaction, complaints and grievances. The purpose is to establish the nature and range of situations that fall into these three broad categories. A consensus will provide you with a good understanding of the range of people's tolerance relative to your working environment and where your interpretations of the above events fit within this range.

The disciplinary process and links to results management

There is discipline in all forms of human life. Within the family unit, within clubs and institutions that people join voluntarily, within organisations and within local and national governments. The queue of people waiting to get into a cinema is a form of discipline. Torrington and Hall (1998) describe discipline as the 'regulation of human activity to produce a controlled performance'.

About discipline

There are two forms of discipline: self-discipline and imposed discipline.

Self-discipline comes from within ourselves. For example, if I were told to run 20 miles, then climb a mountain before cycling for 50 miles because I will enjoy it, my response would undoubtedly be unprintable. But people do such things and voluntarily engage in many other physically and mentally challenging pursuits. It is because they are motivated to participate in such activities, whatever they may be, and possess the self-discipline needed for participation and success. Self-discipline is an invaluable trait to develop and managers' jobs are usually much easier when dealing with self-disciplined staff.

Imposed discipline is that which is imposed by a body or person in, or perceived to be in, a position of control and authority. Imposed discipline is often discharged through written and unwritten laws, regulations, rules and customs by people in authority such as parents, teachers, the police, managers, security guards and bouncers.

At one end of the spectrum are the laws of the land, which apply either to all people or to defined categories of people. At the other end there may be an individual at a gate saying, 'I am sorry, you cannot enter'. People generally accept imposed discipline, provided they agree with the need for it and the rules which uphold the need.

Why have disciplinary processes?

Disciplinary rules and procedures are necessary for promoting orderly employment relations, as well as fairness and consistency in the treatment of individuals. They allow the organisation to get the job done and to operate effectively. They enable organisations to influence the conduct of staff and to deal with problems of poor performance and attendance. They also ensure that employers comply with the law.

A disciplined employee is one who knows where their boundaries lie and normally operates within them, so it is essential that staff know what standards of conduct and performance are expected of them. In the UK, the Employment Rights Act 1996 requires employers to provide written information for their staff about certain aspects of its disciplinary rules and procedures. You should be familiar with these rules and procedures.

The manager's role

It is a mistake to think that managers only deal with the negative aspects of discipline, such as disciplining staff who are underperforming or who have transgressed rules and regulations. Much of the modern manager's role should involve providing the resources and conditions to enable teams to become self-disciplined, self-motivated and to take on greater autonomy, responsibility and wider powers of decision making. These initiatives are all designed to improve people's jobs and improve the intrinsic satisfiers of their jobs.

However, you are responsible for taking appropriate actions, including disciplinary action against your staff, but you should not act alone or without reference to your organisation's policy. Organisations typically have staged disciplinary responses, which involve other senior managers and the HR department.

Torrington and Hall (1998) outline disciplinary responses and the managers likely to be involved at each stage. See Figure 4.1.

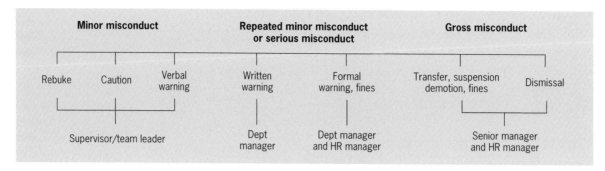

Figure 4.1 *Outline disciplinary procedure*

Source: *Adapted from Torrington and Hall* (1998)

There is nothing new about people transgressing rules or regulations, or performing poorly. You have to deal with such situations positively, fairly and quickly. In this respect, there are distinct parallels between disciplinary processes and grievance processes. Another parallel with grievance processes is the escalating seriousness of issues and the manner in which you should deal with them. The organisation should adopt a matched response to the relative seriousness of the occurrence of indiscipline.

Taking disciplinary action

Before deciding to take disciplinary action against an individual, you should first be clear that this is the right remedy. You can only understand whether disciplinary action is appropriate if you fully investigate the circumstances surrounding the alleged indiscipline. Are you dealing with the cause or the effect? Is the cause organisation-orientated, rather than person-orientated? In other words, is someone facing the possibility of disciplinary action when it is really the organisation (or you) that is at fault?

> For example, an individual is performing poorly. You may feel that it is a matter of indiscipline because this person attended the same training course as the rest of the group, and they are all performing well. However, you may then recognise that the person did not have the opportunity to practise the new skills after the training course, which was some time ago now. Besides that, you also recognise that making comparisons with the rest of the group is not always valid – people learn at different rates, have different capabilities and different levels of confidence. Perhaps the problem is that you failed to give adequate support?

Your key aim must be to deal with the incident and the individual concerned quickly, fairly and appropriately. If not, other staff will feel that the person 'is getting away with this' or that 'this manager is not in control', and this may damage your standing and working relationships.

Provided you are consistent and are seen to be fair in your handling of disciplinary problems, other managers and staff will support you in your actions.

Dealing with poor performance

Organisations have a right to expect that staff will perform satisfactorily. Standards of performance should be defined clearly and staff should be given the development and resources, including adequate working conditions, to enable them to reasonably meet these standards. When an individual is found to be performing unsatisfactorily, you will need to take action. The following guidelines may help.

Guidelines for dealing with poor performance

- Determine the reasons for poor performance – are they within the individual's control or are there other reasons? Make sure you are dealing with the cause and not the effects.
- Inform the individual that their performance needs to improve.
- Give the person a level of performance that must be reached and maintained.
- Allocate a reasonable timescale for the desired improvement in performance.
- Agree interim goals so that progress can be measured and corrective actions can be taken if necessary.
- Confirm the measurement criteria for the desired standard of performance that must be reached and against which the person's performance will be measured.
- Consider retraining or extra training for the individual.
- Spend some time coaching and encouraging the individual.
- Utilise the contributions of other team members to help the individual improve.

If the reason for poor performance is negligence or lack of application, it may be appropriate to implement disciplinary action. If this is the case, the above guidelines may still be usefully applied on the basis that the disciplinary action has dealt with the past and the above actions will deal with the future.

Dealing with misconduct

Quite separate from their effectiveness in performing their duties, employees are expected to conduct themselves in accordance with the organisation's standards of behaviour. These may be explicit, in the form of specific and sometimes exhaustive rules, or implicitly expressed in terms of more general principles. Either way, these standards will be referred to in the formal disciplinary procedure, which will make clear the type of action that offenders can expect.

Misconduct

Organisations expect employees to follow all their rules but some rules are considered more important than others. So when employees break some codes of behaviour they are allowed a second chance. For example:

- attendance
- punctuality
- dress codes
- health and safety procedures
- minor damage/loss.

In these situations managers are expected to follow a similar course of events to that set out in the section 'Guidelines for dealing with poor performance'. Only cases of persistent misconduct would result in dismissal as a last resort in the disciplinary procedure.

Gross misconduct

Some rules are so fundamental that to breach them, even once, would totally destroy the relationship of trust between employer and employee, to the extent that the employer would find it unacceptable for the employee to continue working in the organisation. The employer may see no alternative but to terminate the relationship immediately. Here are some examples:

- theft, fraud and deliberate falsification of records
- physical violence, serious bullying or harassment
- deliberate damage to property, misuse of an organisation's property, name or brand, or bringing the organisation or its staff into serious disrepute
- negligence which causes or might cause unacceptable loss, damage or injury, or infringement of health and safety rules
- incapability while at work due to drink or drugs
- serious insubordination
- serious breach of confidence.

Some of these examples, such as theft and physical violence, would probably result in the dismissal of any type of employee in virtually any working environment. Others may be less clear-cut. Most airline passengers would expect their pilot to be absolutely sober at all times and therefore airlines tend to be unforgiving of any pilot with the merest hint of alcohol on the breath. On the other hand, a company might take a more lenient view of a sales executive found to be intoxicated after wining and dining a key client.

Gross misconduct is usually relative to the environment in which the individual operates, for example, in an office an individual may have a core duty of confidentiality, whereas a worker on an oil rig has a core duty of safety. But the standards of behaviour expected in your organisation may differ significantly even from similar organisations in your sector.

Essential features of disciplinary procedures

To be effective and to protect the interests of both the organisation and staff, an organisation's disciplinary procedures should:

- be in writing
- specify to whom they apply
- be non-discriminatory
- provide for matters to be dealt with promptly
- provide for proceedings, witness statements and records to be kept confidential
- indicate the disciplinary actions that might be taken
- specify the levels of management that have the authority to take the various forms of disciplinary action
- provide for staff to be informed of the complaints against them and, where possible, all relevant evidence before any hearing
- provide staff with an opportunity to state their case before decisions are reached
- provide staff with the right to be accompanied to any interviews (note statutory or regulatory rights in these areas)
- ensure that, except for acts of gross misconduct, staff are not dismissed for a first breach of discipline
- ensure that disciplinary action is not taken until the case has been investigated fully
- ensure that staff are given an explanation of any penalties imposed
- provide a right of appeal to a senior manager and specify the process to be followed.

Stages in the disciplinary process

Informal rebukes and cautions

Rebukes and cautions are part of the everyday life of work and serve to keep people on track. Their nature is often defined by:

◆ the informal setting and delivery

◆ the formality of the message

◆ the immediacy of the rebuke or caution to the incident.

A rebuke is often a reminder about rules, whereas a caution deals with a slightly more serious misdemeanour, for example the deliberate breaking of a rule that requires a formal response from the team leader. You may explain that future actions or sanctions might be taken against the individual if further transgressions occur.

You will probably issue rebukes and cautions in the hope that they will be sufficient to motivate the individual to perform better and to deter the individual from repeating the misdemeanour. When cautioning individuals, you may also indicate what might happen should the individual re-offend.

You may choose to issue a long series of such rebukes and cautions but until you have placed your foot on the first step of the formal disciplinary procedure escalator, your actions still remain resolutely informal. However long the informal stage, this will not cut short the formal procedure, which must take its due course to be legally fair.

Keeping notes. It is important to maintain notes on staff performance in the normal course of your work, and it is also recommended that you make a note of any informal cautions given. When you are next reviewing the individual's performance, you may feel it is worth informing them of your pleasure at the change or improvement in their performance that has resulted from the caution. However, be aware that under the Data Protection Act the individual may have the right to disclosure of any notes that you keep on them in your own files as well as those kept on HR files. So any statements should be capable of bearing public scrutiny.

Disciplinary interviews

Disciplinary interviews are difficult occasions for managers as well as the offending member of staff. Therefore, a good process for conducting interviews helps greatly in what can sometimes be highly charged, emotional, frustrating or angry situations.

When dealing with minor disciplinary breaches, you may elect to deal with them in a low-key way, by conducting an informal meeting or counselling session in which you state the reasons for the meeting and your views, and ask the individual to respond. Such meetings often conclude with the manager reiterating the possibility of disciplinary action being taken if more transgressions occur and with agreement on future performance.

In a case of alleged gross misconduct the employer is claiming that the employee's behaviour is so serious it has destroyed the contract between them, and the employee should be dismissed immediately. However, it would be unfair to do so without an investigation and a formal hearing, so the employer cannot 'instantly dismiss'. After all the employee may be wrongly accused and this may be the outcome of the investigation, which is usually conducted by a third party from HR. Therefore the employee has to remain employed until the due process is complete. But in the meantime, the employer cannot let the employee return to work as normal without implying that perhaps the misconduct wasn't really serious enough to warrant dismissal. There is, then, only one realistic option. It is normal for employers wishing to avoid the risk of losing an unfair dismissal claim, to suspend, on full pay, any employees accused of gross misconduct pending the outcome of the procedure. If the employee is innocent then they can return to work without financial penalty. If guilty, the employer is not compromised.

For any formal disciplinary interview, you may want a member of the HR team to be present. The interview might include the following elements and actions.

Before the meeting:

♦ Make sure all investigations are concluded and that you and any other managerial staff attending are aware of all the facts and issues involved in the case.

♦ Write to the individual setting out the charge against them.

♦ Confirm the time and venue – book the room.

♦ Notify employee of location and time.

♦ Advise employee of right to be accompanied at the meeting.

♦ Notify witnesses and confirm their attendance (if appropriate).

♦ Maintain contact with the HR department, which provides advice and support. In some cases the HR department may write the warnings and advise on the alternatives open to you.

At the meeting:

♦ Thank people for attending and outline the structure of the meeting.

♦ State the reason why everyone is present and ask the employee if they understand why they are at the meeting.

♦ Present the facts of the case and call any witnesses to support the case.

- Ask the employee to respond – they may wish to question the witnesses.

- Adjourn to consider your decision – to announce your decision immediately looks like you have already made up your mind.

Reconvene the meeting:

- Announce your decision, for example, that the negligence has been proved and that you are issuing a warning under the organisation's disciplinary procedure.

- Explain that if any further incidents occur, further disciplinary action of a more serious nature will be taken against the individual.

- If the individual is to be dismissed, explain that dismissal is immediate.

Note that in some cases it may not be in an organisation's interests to allow a dismissed member of staff back into the workplace. In such cases, individuals should be escorted from the premises.

After the meeting:

- Make a note of actions taken at the meeting and forward a copy to the HR department.

- Send the individual a written copy of your decision if you have not already provided this at the meeting. This document should confirm that a warning has been issued, the reasons why it has been issued and that if similar incidents occur, further and more serious disciplinary action may be taken. The document might also contain specific information on performance criteria that the individual must meet, for example timekeeping, attendance at work.

The individual may decide to appeal against the decision taken at the meeting and they should be advised of the appeals process. Taking disciplinary action is not an easy matter for managers to deal with – the organisation's policy and procedures should provide a framework of support to make the process easier.

Sanctions

1 Warnings

Warnings form the starting point of many organisational disciplinary processes. Pay careful attention to the process and your role in the process, as you may be held accountable at higher forums, for example employment tribunals. Above all else, you and other involved managers must deal fairly with the individual. Seek the advice of the HR specialist when contemplating issuing a warning to an individual to ensure that standards are maintained and that equitable treatment is given.

If you issue a verbal warning, you should confirm this in writing and include:

- the date and the place where the performance issue or incident occurred
- the nature of the performance issue or incident
- the action which may be taken if the performance issue is unresolved or the incident is repeated
- information that failure to improve performance or further repetition of the incident could lead to other penalties, which may include suspension or dismissal
- confirmation that this is the first stage in the organisation's formal disciplinary process.

2 Transfer, suspension, demotion or fines

An organisation may apply one or all of these penalties, depending on the seriousness of the offence. However, you should take care to check that the sanction you propose to take is permitted under your organisation's procedure, otherwise you risk being in breach of contract. The characteristics of these penalties are that they are public and that people understand why they have been applied. The problem with them is the resentment that they can cause in the recipient. People often resign rather than face the ignominy of transfer, suspension or demotion. Note that in this context, 'suspension' refers to a punishment, not to a suspension imposed while an investigation is conducted.

3 Dismissal

Employees can be dismissed fairly for a number of reasons other than poor performance or incapability, or conduct:

- Redundancy – where you cease to have a requirement for a particular type of work
- Lack of qualification – for example where you discover an employee does not have the qualifications claimed on their CV
- Where employment would break the law – for example, no work permit
- Some other substantial reason.

Whatever the reason, the decision to dismiss must never be taken lightly because of the implications, not just for the individual concerned, but also for their dependants. Taking away an individual's livelihood is a serious matter. However, that should not deter managers and organisations from acting appropriately where the need arises.

Activity 13
Discipline

Objective

This activity will help you to match your reactions regarding appropriate disciplinary actions to incidents that typically occur within organisations.

Task

Here we take a brief look at some typical disciplinary situations. The nature of discipline is very particular to the individuals concerned and the environment in which they operate. In the chart we provide some typical examples of indiscipline by staff in different environments and leave you to make your own connections.

1 Confirm your understanding of your organisation's disciplinary policy and processes before comparing them with the generic incidents and responses we give in the examples.

2 Determine which of the following options for disciplinary action you/ your organisation would take in the following circumstances and, in so doing, think about the reasoning which lies behind your decisions:

R	rebuke	F	formal warning
C	caution	T/S/F	transfer/suspension/fine
V	verbal warning	D	dismissal
W	written warning		

Occurrence	Your/your organisation's response
1 Jim was late for work, and missed a meeting at which it was important he contribute his knowledge and views – he does not have a reasonable excuse for his lateness	
2 Sarah has made several errors in her work over a period of a few weeks that have caused problems for her internal customers. You have already had a word with her about this. She has the skills and knowledge to perform better	
3 It is Grant's responsibility to check the fire extinguishers every month. You discover that they have not been checked for three months and he has no excuses when you discuss this with him	
4 Three wallets have been stolen from handbags and jackets. It appears that Sophie was the only person in the office at the time they went missing	

Occurrence	Your/your organisation's response
5 On a regular check of staff cars, Jim was caught removing components from the company premises for which he had no authority or need in connection with his work	
6 Jill never seems to be around when she is needed. She always has an excuse for her absences, but you know she spends a lot of time chatting with her friends in the neighbouring department	
7 Fred is a troublemaker. He constantly complains about minor issues that he always tries to make bigger than they are. In so doing, he spends too much time arguing with team members and managers rather than doing his job	
8 Gemma has already had two verbal warnings about her failure to wear safety clothing at all times. She says she looks and feels ridiculous in the clothing	
9 A company check on Internet usage reveals that Sanjit spends approximately two hours per day surfing the Net, but not in connection with his job	
10 Jim and Roy have a serious, long-running personal disagreement and have nearly come to blows on several occasions. Despite being warned, they have failed to resolve their differences, and their negativity towards each other is having a significant effect on team morale and effectiveness	
11 Blossom's desk is always very untidy – she can never find anything when you ask her for it	
12 The report that Andrew should have provided is now three days late – you have already asked for it twice	
13 Despite the company circular and verbal reminders to all staff, George still doesn't turn off his PC before going home	
14 Philip failed to ensure that a hole on the site was correctly cordoned off and marked with a danger sign. A lorry reversed into the hole, spilling its load and damaging the vehicle. The driver had to be taken to hospital with serious head and back injuries	

Feedback

Naturally, there is a range of responses you might make. The common denominator is that you would need to know more about the individuals and the occurrences before arriving at a decision. For example, in No. 12, if Andrew is normally a very reliable employee, what is preventing him from completing the report? We have provided our responses below with some rationale and we acknowledge that your responses may differ.

1   Caution
    It was important that Jim attend the meeting. He has not only let himself down, but also the other people who took the trouble to attend the meeting, including you. His absence should not be tolerated.

2   Verbal warning
    Your previous informal attempts to persuade Sarah to perform better have not had the desired effect. She should now understand the seriousness of her errors.

3 Formal warning
Grant must understand the seriousness of his omissions. He has compromised staff safety.

4 Suspension or temporary transfer
There is no proof that Sophie has taken the wallets. The organisation should ask the local police to investigate. Suspension without prejudice may be the only immediate action the organisation can take, but even this may be inadvisable. A temporary transfer may be in order, but suspension or transfer may raise perceptions of guilt, against which Sophie may take civil action.

5 Dismissal
Stealing is a very serious offence. Summary dismissal is the right disciplinary action to take.

6 Rebuke or caution
Jill needs to be reminded of her responsibilities; a rebuke may be all that is required. Specific instances of her absence causing problems should be made at the time the rebuke or caution is issued.

7 Caution
Fred's demeanour should be brought to his attention. There may be underlying reasons which you should try to find out in a meeting. If there are no underlying reasons, a strong caution should be issued.

8 Written warning
The safety clothing is to be worn for good reasons – possibly regulatory. Gemma must be left in no doubt that continued behaviour of this kind will not be tolerated.

9 Dismissal or formal warning
This could be a dismissal offence if there is a clear company policy against unauthorised use of the Internet. At minimum, Sanjit should receive a formal warning. He is being unproductive for two hours per day and he is leaving it open to serious question as to whether the company needs to retain his services.

10 Written warnings or transfers
Both individuals must understand that their behaviour is affecting team performance and morale. One or both may be transferred.

11 Rebuke
A pointed reminder to Blossom may be all that is needed – she should also be informed that you will be keeping an eye on her and her desk.

12   Rebuke or caution
     Maybe. You should find out why Andrew hasn't given you the
     report and rebuke him for not keeping you informed. He may
     be waiting for information from another department and
     your assistance might help. However, if there is no good
     reason for the lateness, then a caution might be merited.

13   Caution
     There is no excuse for this behaviour. A strong caution
     should be issued.

14   Suspension
     No immediate disciplinary action should be taken. An
     investigation should be held – maybe involving the health and
     safety regulatory body. Suspension without prejudice is the
     correct action in the circumstances. Philip should be advised
     of his rights and asked to assist any investigation.

You may also wish to discuss this activity with your colleagues.
When contemplating or taking disciplinary action, it is important
for managers and organisations to adopt a fair and consistent
approach.

◆ Recap

This theme has looked at the formal processes available to you to
deal with poor performance and achieve results.

**Explore how the grievance process operates in your organisation
to help you deal with conflict or poor quality of work**

◆ It is important to distinguish between dissatisfactions,
  complaints and grievances. They all need to be dealt with in
  different ways.

◆ You need to be clear about the processes in place to deal with
  harassment, bullying and constructive dismissal.

◆ Your role is to take appropriate action to prevent poor morale
  and employee relations difficulties.

**Explore the way in which the disciplinary process operates in
your organisation and find ways to deal with disciplinary
matters promptly and effectively**

◆ Discipline is about self-discipline and imposed discipline.

◆ Rules and procedures are required to promote orderly
  employment relations as well as fairness and consistency in the
  treatment of individuals.

◆ The manager's role should include providing the resources and conditions to enable teams to become self-disciplined.

Identify situations in which an informal approach to discipline is effective and when to use the formal procedures

◆ Guidelines are provided for dealing with poor performance as well as dealing with misconduct and gross misconduct.

◆ The essential features of disciplinary procedures are outlined, as are the use of rebukes and cautions. A range of situations illustrate how these approaches translate into the overall picture of the disciplinary process.

Find out how to conduct a formal disciplinary interview

◆ Disciplinary interviews are difficult occasions for managers as well as the member of staff being disciplined.

◆ They can be dealt with in a low-key way, but whether dealt with formally or informally the need to make notes and agree actions is fundamental.

◆ Guidance is provided on what to do before the meeting, at the meeting and after the meeting.

▶▶ More @

Stredwick, J. (2000) *An Introduction to Human Resource Management*, Elsevier Butterworth-Heinemann
A comprehensive and wide-ranging text which examines all the major aspects of human resource management in a down-to-earth and practical way. Chapter 7 focuses on relationships with employees and in particular dealing with group and individual sources of conflict, grievance and discipline.

Thomson, R. (2002) 3rd edition, *Managing People*, Elsevier Butterworth-Heinemann
Managing People addresses the perspective of the individual manager whose role includes the management of people, as well as issues concerning the organisation as a whole. See particularly Chapter 9, Managing challenging situations, and Chapter 10 'The regulation of behaviour at work' for useful guidance on all aspects of diversity, discipline, power, stress and dismissal.

Torrington, D. and Hall, L. (1998) 5th edition, *Human Resource Management*, FT Prentice Hall
This book is written from a practical management perspective. It includes full coverage of operational issues and introduces the major academic debates of relevance to the field. The book is divided into

six core parts focusing on strategy, operations and skills. This fifth edition has been fully updated to take account of developments in professional thinking, academic research and employment legislation. It includes information on handling grievance and disciplinary processes.

Tyson, S. and York, A. (2000) 4th edition, *Essentials of HRM*, Elsevier Butterworth-Heinemann

Essentials of HRM combines an overview of organisational behaviour with a detailed explanation of human resource management policies and techniques. It also acts as an introduction to the study of industrial relations. This book covers this theme in a section entitled, 'Industrial relations'. It includes useful sections on negotiation techniques, disputes and ways of resolving conflict and employment law in Chapters 18, 19 and 21.

www.acas.org.uk and www.dti.gov.uk

ACAS, the UK arbitration service, has some useful material on its website, www.acas.org.uk, in particular a self-help guide entitled 'Producing disciplinary and grievance procedures'. In the UK, the government website www.dti.gov.uk has some reference material and links.

Full references are provided at the end of the book.

5 A balancing act

As a manager you have to balance a range of sometimes conflicting needs in order to achieve the results you require. This theme looks at how far to retain control when delegating, when to allocate tasks or to agree them, and ways of working with individuals in a team situation.

You will be able to determine your preferred leadership style and whether it is appropriate for your role as an effective results manager, and reflect on your approach to briefing the team.

This theme sets a framework to help you balance conflicting needs. You will:

♦ **Review your approach to the needs of team members and the support they require**

♦ **Explore issues around the control of work and empowering people to develop their own ways of working**

♦ **Identify ways of getting employees to take a lead in their areas of expertise on the results they are asked to deliver.**

Balancing needs and achieving results

As a manager you constantly have to balance the needs of teams and of individuals, and the needs of the task itself – all within the context and culture of the organisation. In managing for results, one or more of these needs may be paramount, and you have to deal with particular situations, while bearing in mind their impact on the other areas of need – see Figure 5.1.

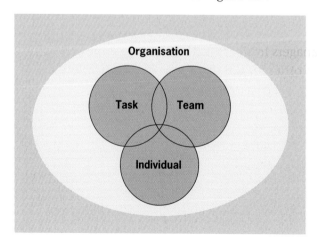

Figure 5.1 *The range of needs managers must meet*

Examples of how different needs may come to the fore
To complete the task, the team needs to be issued with special safety clothing, which has been ordered but not yet arrived. **(Team needs)**

Members of the team need to be trained in how to operate the new equipment before operations begin. **(Individual/team needs)**

A key specialist has unexpectedly asked for time off work to be approved because his wife is ill. **(Individual needs)**

Individuals are keen to maintain their open learning development programmes, but the task is interfering with their learning. **(Individual/task needs)**

The delivery deadline to the client will not be met unless individual productivity improves and the team works overtime. **(Task/team/individual needs)**

Getting the balance right is not always straightforward and, in difficult situations, you could discuss options with your boss, customers (especially internal) and your team. You should only discuss options with your external customers if you know that whatever is or is not occurring will affect them directly.

Teams versus individuals

We already know that a high-performing team can produce synergistic results, with everyone committed towards the goal. However, in being committed to the goal, the high-performing team also has an understanding of the needs of individuals within the team, for if these individual needs are not addressed, they will detract from individual and overall team effectiveness. Take the following example:

A group of six managers from across the country, some of whom were meeting each other for the first time, were on a voluntary team-building course. One activity was to navigate their way through woods and across some low hills on an orienteering exercise, gathering information and clues along the way which would enable them to complete the next activity. No leader was appointed or elected and the group set off.

Three other groups were also undertaking this exercise, but starting from different locations. The managers assumed it was a competition.

About 40 minutes into the activity, one of the managers twisted his ankle and had trouble walking on the rough terrain. Two other members of the group suggested leaving him there, but the others weren't keen. One manager suggested they all walk at the pace of the injured man and everyone agreed.

While walking along, another manager said, 'How do we know this is a competition?' This question sparked off a great debate and the managers concluded that it was not a competition. They collected information from three checkpoints and were on the way to the fourth when they met another group coming towards them. The two groups decided to exchange information and they repeated this process with the other two groups. The net result was that the four groups completed the activity in a much shorter time than they had anticipated.

At the debriefing session, the managers all confirmed that they had started off by thinking it was a competitive activity. It was only because one group had to address the overriding needs of an individual, that another manager took the time to think through what they had been asked to do. By correctly addressing the needs of the individual, the four groups acted as one team, rather than as four disparate and competitive groups.

Control versus delegation

The Tannenbaum and Schmidt (1973) model of autocratic versus democratic leadership, shown in Figure 5.2, provides a good insight into the different approaches which managers can take to people and situations.

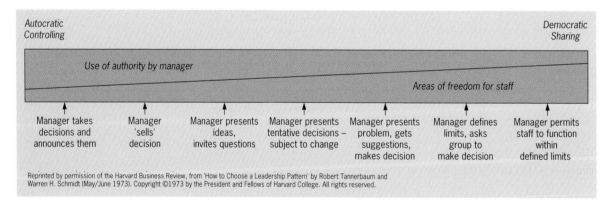

Figure 5.2 *The leadership continuum*

Source: *Tannenbaum and Schmidt* (1973)

You can use this model by asking: 'What leadership approach should I take in this situation, and with the people involved, to achieve the best results for the organisation and the people involved?' In asking this question you might find yourself with incompatible answers, as shown in the example below.

The result the company wants is to shift orders to customers by staff working overtime for the next five days to clear the backlog.

The result staff want is to do the overtime, but not commit to five straight days, as this will have a significant impact on personal and family lives.

Is there middle ground? Can you achieve an equitable result that meets both sets of needs? The answer is probably yes, but it will depend very much on the interaction of the company, the manager, the staff and the situation. See Figure 5.3.

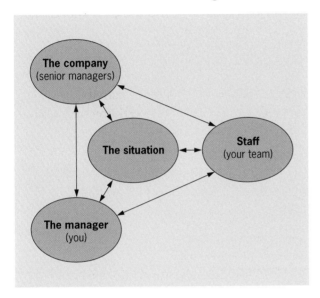

Figure 5.3 *Interaction to get results*

Ideally, you are acting as the focal point on important issues, but you should also be confident enough in yourself and your team to encourage direct dialogue between the team, or selected members of the team, and involved senior managers, for example, the project sponsor, department head, divisional director.

The only problem in agreeing certain team members as conduits is that senior managers often have a habit of talking with whoever they can get hold of, if they need fast or urgent access to information. It may be in your best interests to encourage a free dialogue and take steps to ensure that you are kept informed.

To resolve the two apparently incompatible issues in the example above, you could contact the distribution department and get them to ask the involved customers if they really need all of their orders within the next five days, or what proportion of their orders they need. This might prompt a more accurate response of customers' needs, which will mean staff working overtime over a longer period, but which will accommodate individual needs. This is a flexible response that maintains balance between needs and outcomes. However, you could take matters further in determining how far you are prepared to control the overtime working. You could:

- tell staff when they have to work overtime

- suggest to staff when they have to work overtime, and ask for their responses

- ask staff to volunteer for overtime, and say that you might need to adjust the roster if gaps appear

- ask staff to sort out the overtime roster and present it to you, but if they have any problems they should discuss these with you before finalising the roster

- ask staff to resolve it themselves – this means that they are involved in problem solving and decision making, and are much more likely to work the overtime.

By involving staff in the decision, you are likely to find that they will be more committed to the overtime, and the backlog could be cleared quicker than anticipated.

Here you have a range of responses that span the control versus delegation continuum shown in Figure 5.2. All are valid leadership approaches, but the approach you take may be based upon a combination of:

- the culture of the organisation
- your preferred style of leadership
- your confidence in, and respect for, the staff and your perception of their ability to contribute to, or resolve, the situation
- the time pressure you are experiencing.

There are some circumstances when retaining tight control of staff is appropriate, but managers' jobs are becoming bigger and busier and they are less able to exercise this level of control on a regular basis.

Delegation to staff is a sign of good, strong leadership provided the delegation is handled correctly. Delegation should provide some of Herzberg's intrinsic satisfiers – more challenging work, more variety in jobs, greater responsibility – and this can serve to build confidence and commitment among your team members.

Allocating versus agreeing tasks

You may know the results you need to achieve, but do you know the best way to get there?

It is often beneficial to involve the people who are going to perform a task in planning and agreeing it. Bear in mind that nobody knows a job better than the people who do it, day in, day out.

A house construction company had planning permission to build a group of new houses on a greenfield site, which had a very narrow access road and a tight turning at the end of the lane into the site. All materials had to pass down this road and there were fixed restrictions on both sides. The managers were particularly concerned about trucks carrying the large and unwieldy prefabricated units onto the site. They studied and restudied the building plans and considered smaller fabrications, but the architect said that would be a very expensive option.

When one of the managers visited another site, he was asked by three construction workers how planning was going for the new site. The manager said the start date might be delayed because of access problems. Quizzed further, the manager outlined the problems. One of the construction workers suggested they use a crane to lift the large fabrications into the site from the other side. All the company would have to do was lay a portable steel roadway across a field for the crane and the delivery trucks. The crane would then lift the units over a row of buildings and place them on the site. A smaller crane could then move the units into position on the site.

Many organisations throughout the world practise total quality (TQ) or continuous improvement (CI) as it is sometimes known. A cornerstone of TQ/CI is that every person involved in a process or part of a process is always looking at a more effective way of undertaking it. So, if tasks are allocated, the expectation is that team members will still look for a better way of undertaking them. However, within such organisations, the trend is very much towards agreeing the task and the process.

If you tell someone precisely what to do, are you taking away their freedom to understand the purpose of the task and to do the task in the best way? As long as the end results meet all required standards, can you give team members autonomy in the manner in which they carry out the tasks? The greater the autonomy, the greater the motivation towards the task.

Some tasks may have strict controls and sequencing, for example stage 1 must be completed before stage 2, but with some thought and ingenuity, it may be possible to change the sequencing so that tasks can be undertaken concurrently, or dependencies may be changed. It may also be possible to brief team members about the constraints and requirements they must meet in performing the task.

Giving people time

Spend time with your team members, getting to know them, coaching and encouraging them. You must also spend time with them to gain feedback on a wide range of issues affecting their jobs, including progress on goals and objectives.

By getting to know people, you are better placed to make judgements about their capabilities, levels of potential and possible areas for development. This can help you when matching a task or role to an individual.

There will always be times in your work as a manager when you have to make a decision on whether team issues or individual issues are paramount and therefore more deserving of your time than other issues. Whatever decision you make, keep in mind the overall results that you wish to achieve. It is very easy to become distracted, especially on people issues, and lose sight of the objective.

Setting or agreeing objectives

If you allocate work, you are likely to set objectives. If you are able to agree tasks with people, you can ask them to draft their own objectives, and then review and agree them together. By encouraging people to take some responsibility for setting and agreeing their objectives, you are enhancing their commitment, or buy-in, to achieving them.

When asking people to draft their own objectives, make sure that they have the information they need. For example, they should be linked directly to achieving the overall business results; they may need to meet certain constraints in terms of resource availability and deadlines. Make sure your people know how to write objectives that are SMART.

SMART objectives are:

- Specific – it is clear what needs to be achieved
- Measurable – so it is clear when it has been achieved
- Achievable – with the resources available
- Results-orientated – so the outcomes required are clearly stated, rather than the process for achieving them
- Time-bound – with appropriate deadlines for interim checking and completion.

Of course, objectives are only good for the day on which they are agreed. Life moves on and anything might occur which renders an objective obsolete or impossible to achieve. It is important to review objectives regularly to ensure they remain valid.

Team briefings

Team briefings form an important communications channel in many organisations, enabling information to flow down the organisation to team level and then back up in the form of feedback from individuals and teams. Their purpose is to encourage participation and commitment. There is no set pattern or format for team briefings, but typically they include the characteristics or features set out in Table 5.1.

	Characteristics
Frequency	Held regularly, depending on the needs of the individuals, manager and team, and on the range of topics covered
People involved	Team leader or manager and all team members
	There is often a process to inform people who miss a team briefing or who are off-site, to enable them to respond
	People from outside the team may be invited to attend and speak, for example HR staff, staff from other departments or teams
Format	Generally follow a common format within the organisation or division
	Organisations often publish core information to be communicated at team briefings at all levels – to ensure consistency of the message and completeness of coverage
	Often start with team leader or manager providing information on organisational issues; team members can then respond or mention other topics
	Brief – perhaps lasting for no more than 30 minutes
	The team leader or manager listens more than talks (80/20)

Table 5.1 *Characteristics of a team briefing*

The Industrial Society (1990) was important in pioneering team briefings and it suggests that briefings should include the following:

Progress:	How we are doing – the progress of the company, division, department and team
People:	Who is coming and going
Policy:	Any changes affecting the team
Points:	For further action

Source: *Wintour* (1990)

People – a process improvement approach

We have already mentioned the balance between delegation and control. A process improvement approach takes this a step further. Consider this as the future of organisational life.

There are fewer managers and therefore fewer layers of management. Teams of people work across a wide range of tasks without direct manager involvement, but after agreeing objectives and priorities with their managers. Every week the teams hold meetings. Often there is no manager present as they can't cover all of their teams' meetings at one time. The teams have no nominated leader – whatever needs to be done is done and the teams operate on a consensus basis to ensure they achieve the results required by the organisation.

Each member of the team is a specialist in one or more areas, or if more than two people with the same skills and similar experience are on a team, they are allocated specific areas of responsibility. However, it is common to see them helping each other, or working on tasks which have been allocated to another individual. If people have completed their tasks or have spare time, they help others. They don't need to be asked, it is just what happens within the teams.

People come and go as the teams reform, because of new or changed tasks. The organisation is great at developing people and has a policy to maintain employment whenever possible. Everyone understands that being in work is more important than being in a job. If people are asked to move, they do so on the understanding that it is intended to keep them in work, and that their skills and experience will be utilised or they will be retrained to acquire new skills. A by-product is that multiskilling is commonplace, and the workforce can be utilised in a far more flexible manner than previously.

The organisation is very customer focused and allocates a large number of resources to research and development. It has seen its position in its markets improve year on year for the past five years, and its brand is now recognised as a market leader.

This form of working is here today in many organisations that are reshaping to cope with the highly competitive markets in which they operate. Staff are given responsibility for, and take ownership of, their operations. This means the following:

- They are responsible for the inputs to, the conversion and the outputs from their processes

- In being responsible for the inputs, they have to maintain open communications with their suppliers – whether they are internal or external

- In being responsible for their outputs, they have to maintain open communications with their customers – whether they are internal or external

- They operate on the basis that everyone is someone else's customer

- They are continually working to improve processes and outputs.

What does all this mean for you as a manager? You have the responsibility to create the conditions and to empower people to work in this way. It is you who agree the standards and results that must be achieved. You are responsible for enabling people to give of their best, but this must be on a continuous basis, not just by speaking or being available every now and again.

You can empower people by giving them challenging jobs with variety and autonomy. You can help them to develop their skills, so that they are motivated to contribute positively to the organisation.

Activity 14
Balancing needs and achieving results

Objectives

This activity will help you to:

- determine your preferred leadership style and whether it is appropriate for your role as an effective results manager

- reflect on your approach to briefing the team.

Task

1 Reflect on a recent situation where you had to lead a discussion or brief your team. Then answer the following questions.

Using the scale shown in Tannenbaum and Schmidt's model, Figure 5.2, where would you place yourself on the scale of 'sharing' to 'controlling'?

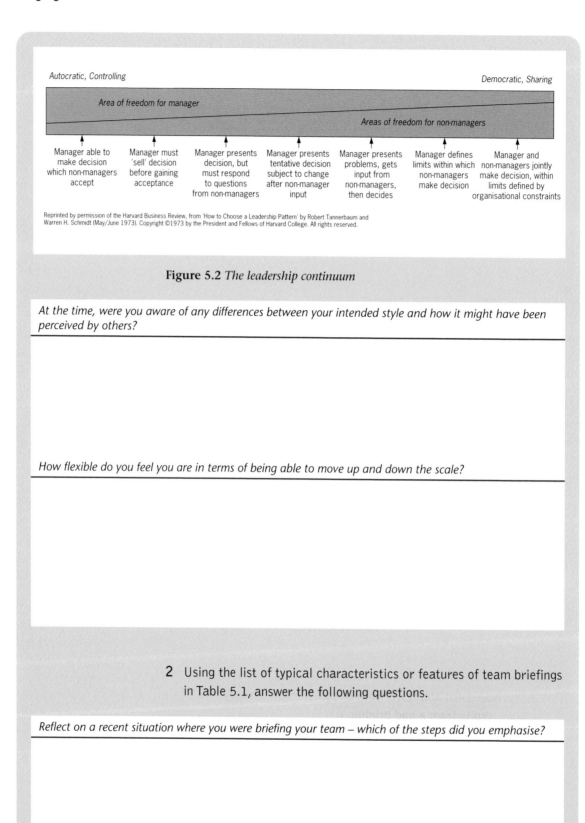

Autocratic, Controlling   *Democratic, Sharing*

Area of freedom for manager

Areas of freedom for non-managers

| Manager able to make decision which non-managers accept | Manager must 'sell' decision before gaining acceptance | Manager presents decision, but must respond to questions from non-managers | Manager presents tentative decision subject to change after non-manager input | Manager presents problems, gets input from non-managers, then decides | Manager defines limits within which non-managers make decision | Manager and non-managers jointly make decision, within limits defined by organisational constraints |

Reprinted by permission of the Harvard Business Review, from 'How to Choose a Leadership Pattern' by Robert Tannerbaum and Warren H. Schmidt (May/June 1973). Copyright ©1973 by the President and Fellows of Harvard College. All rights reserved.

Figure 5.2 *The leadership continuum*

At the time, were you aware of any differences between your intended style and how it might have been perceived by others?

How flexible do you feel you are in terms of being able to move up and down the scale?

2 Using the list of typical characteristics or features of team briefings in Table 5.1, answer the following questions.

Reflect on a recent situation where you were briefing your team – which of the steps did you emphasise?

Were there any gaps in your briefing and if so, what impact do you believe this had, or is likely to have, on your success in delivering the required results of the task?

Feedback

You probably found that the natural style to adopt is the one that you feel most comfortable with. Changing style to suit the situation is only sensible when your motives are clear to those involved. A manager who offers a chameleon approach soon ceases to have the respect of a team. At times it is vital to take direct control of actions and this is fine as long as the team members know why you have decided to adopt that style.

You may have noticed that other managers offer a consistent style and this becomes a part of their perceived persona. This has advantages, but matching style to intent and to the situation is a skill that needs to be experimented with and then ingrained. In this way your chances of delivering results will be greatly improved.

Briefing a team or an individual is apparently straightforward, but the reality is that most of us are very bad at it. Following a brief and adopting a reflective approach to your efforts will pay dividends. Seek feedback from the team on how effective your briefings have been and learn from this feedback. The wasted time that results from a bad briefing is considerable and will certainly interfere with your attempts to become an effective results manager.

◆ Recap

This theme has explored the difficult decisions you need to take to reconcile sometimes conflicting needs.

Review your approach to the needs of team members and the support they require

♦ Getting the balance right between tasks, teams and individuals can be difficult.

♦ A high performing team, as well as being committed to the task, has an understanding of the needs of individuals within the team.

Explore issues around the control of work and empowering people to develop their own ways of working

♦ Your decisions around control of work are likely to be based on the culture of your organisation, your preferred style of leadership, your confidence and trust in your team and the time pressures you are experiencing.

♦ Delegation and empowerment are signs of good, strong leadership.

Identify ways of getting employees to take a lead in their areas of expertise on the results they are asked to deliver

♦ In order for people to take responsibility, they need to be given time and clear objectives.

♦ A process improvement culture, where employees are the experts in their own area of the process and take responsibility for their operations, may be the way forward.

▶▶ More @

Daniels, A. C. (2000) *Bringing Out the Best in People*, McGraw-Hill
Effective management of personnel leads to outstanding individual performances that, in turn, lead to great organisational performance. This text tells how to initiate organisational change so that employees will increase their efforts, their creativity, their co-operation and quality of work.

Tannenbaum, R. and Schmidt, W. H. (1973) 'How to choose a leadership pattern', *Harvard Business Review*, May/June
This was the original article upon which subsequent research has been based. It outlines the model of leadership based on a continuum from autocratic/controlling to democratic/sharing.

References

Adams, J. S. (1965) 'Inequity in social exchange', in Berkowitz, L. (ed) *Advances in experimental social psychology*, Vol. 2, Academic Press

Bilmes, L. (2001) 'Scoring goals for people and company', in Mastering People Management, *Financial Times*, 26 November

Cates, K. and Rahimi, K. (2001) 'Algebra lessons for older wrokers', in Mastering People Management, *Financial Times*, 19 November

Chartered Institute for Personnel and Development (2001) *Reward Determination in the UK*, CIPD Research Report

Chatman, J. A. and Jehn, K. A. (1994) 'Assessing the relationship between industry characteristics and organisational culture: How different can you be?' *Academy of Management Journal*, 37, p.522–533

Cottell, C. (2001) 'How low will you go to stay in work?' *The Guardian*, 8 December

Crainer, S. (1995) 'Re-engineering the carrot', *Management Today*, December, p.66

Daniels, Aubrey C. (2000) *Bringing Out the Best in People*, McGraw-Hill

Drucker, P. F. (1974) *Management, Tasks, Responsibilities, Practices*, Management Editions (Europe)

Hackman, J. R. and Oldham, G. R. (1980) *Work Redesign*, Addison-Wesley

Handy, C. (2001) *The Elephant and the Flea*, Hutchinson, Random House

Haygroup (2001) www.haygroup.com

Herzberg, F. (1974) *Work and the Nature of Man*, Granada Publishing Ltd

Katzenbach, J. R. and Smith, D. K. (1993) *The Wisdom of Teams*, Harvard Business School Press

Locke, E. A. and Latham, G. P. (1990) *A theory of goal setting and task performance*, Prentice Hall

Manz, C. and Sims, H. P. (1993) *Businesses without Bosses*, John Wiley

Maslow, A. H. (1987) 3rd edition, *Motivation and Personality*, Harper and Row

Mullins, L. J. (1999) 5th edition, *Management and Organisational Behaviour*, FT Pitman Publishing

Nayak, P. R. and Ketteringham, J. M. (1986) *Breakthroughs*, Rawson and Associates

Nike, www.nike.com

Osburn, J. D. L., Musselwhite, E. and Zenger, J. H. (1990) *Self Directed Teams*, Irwin

Pearson, A. W. (1991) 'Managing Innovation: an uncertainty reduction process', in Henry, J. and Walker, D., *Managing Innovation*, Sage Publications

Pigors, P. and Myers, S. (1977) 8th edition, *Personnel Administration*, McGraw-Hill

Porter, L. W. and Lawler, E. E. (1968) *Management Attitudes and Performance*, Irwin

Quinn, J. B. (1986) 'Innovation and corporate strategy: Managed Chaos' in Horwitch, M. (ed) *Technology in the Modern Corporation*, Pergamon Press

Robertson, I. T., Smith, M. and Cooper, D. (1992) 2nd edition, *Motivation, Strategy, Theories and Practice*, Institute of Personnel Management

Rose, M. (2000) *Recognising Performance*, Plymbridge Distributors

Royal Dutch/Shell Group of Companies, www.shell.com

Rucci, A. J., Kirn, S. P. and Quinn, R. T. (1998) 'The employee-customer-profit chain at Sears', *Harvard Business Review*, Jan-Feb

Schein, E. H. (1985) *Organisational Culture and Leadership*, Jossey-Bass

Spitzer, D. R. (1996) 'Power Rewards: rewards that really motivate', *American Management Association Management Review*, May

Tannenbaum, R. and Schmidt, W. H. (1973) 'How to choose a leadership pattern', *Harvard Business Review*, May/June

Torrington, D. and Hall, L. (1998) 4th edition, *Human Resource Management*, Prentice Hall

Vroom, V. H. (1964) *Work and Motivation*, John Wiley

Wellins, R. S., Byham, W. C. and Wilson, J. M. (1991) *Empowered Teams*, Jossey-Bass

Wintour, P. (1990) *A Briefer's Guide to Team Briefing – A Supervisor's Pocket Guide*, The Industrial Society